RAMPAGIN

KATERIN.. NIKULAS

BOOK 2 - the Greek Meze Series

Rampaging Roosters

Katerina Nikolas

Book 2 in The Greek Meze Series

theys no speaks Greek and theys butchers the English" said Adonis, demonstrating his mastery of butchered English.

"Comes my friends tonight we eats together at Yiota's and yous catch up with all old friends in village. Goodly thing is yous 'ouse is still standing. Old Mr Antonopoulos from ups in Katsiki 'ad that new fangled gas put in and 'is 'ouse blew up."

"How dreadful" Deirdre commiserated, mentioning the name sounded familiar.'

"It would do Did-Rees" Adonis agreed, "K-Went-In killed 'is goat and we ate it. Old Mr Antonopoulos 'ad run of badly luck this year."

Quentin peered cautiously over the neighbouring wall and seeing no sign of the old Mercedes taxi he voiced his regret at missing Fotini and Nitsa. "They's out picking up unwilling passengers" Adonis said "that Nitsa not take no for answer."

Chapter 3: Toppling The Ladder

The old crone Fotini was having the time of her life since her second cousin Nitsa came to stay at her home in Rapanaki. With Nitsa's wheels at her disposal she was getting out far more than she had done in years. Creating havoc in the old Mercedes taxi they blatantly ignored the repeated threats of Pancratius the village policeman warning he would be forced to arrest them if they continued extorting extortionate and illegal fares from unwilling passengers, as the taxi was unlicensed.

They had made quite a killing over the tourist season, finding most of their unwilling and very nervous tourist passengers were happy to pay up simply to be released from the back seat, where they were held to ransom by the central locking system. This kept their petrol costs down as they need not drive very far before their passengers demanded to be released, thus bumping up their profit margin nicely.

They felt immune to Pancratius' threats to have them arrested; convinced he was an utterly incompetent hypochondriac. He had miserably failed to solve the case of the intrusive pervert rapist who had broken into Fotini's house and started a potentially lethal fire, and he had also failed to discover the identity of the elusive underwear thief. They played on his fears of a ruined reputation should he be responsible for having two old dears incarcerated in a noxious Greek prison cell.

Prosperous Pedros had told the pair of old crones Quentin and Deirdre were due to arrive back in the village with Quentin's old mother in tow. Fotini and Nitsa were looking forward to making the acquaintance of Hattie, hoping she had a bit more spirit about her than her gormless son. "I 'opes she not so attractive she catch eye of Bald Yannis" said Nitsa, wary of any competition for the attentions of the man she had convinced herself was besotted with her.

"I thoughts yous gone off 'im since he lost terrible toupee" Fotini said.

"Is true 'e is pretty ugly without 'is 'air but yous 'ave to admit Fotini that pickings round 'ere is thin when it comes to admiring men. At least Bald Yannis is young enough to give me good time. That old fool Vasilis is our age and look at state of 'im" Nitsa declared.

"That 'cos mail order hussy wears 'im out with Viagra trying to get herself pregnant, an' he thin as rake from eating 'er disgusting borscht" Fotini said. "I is amazed he took 'er back after way she was carrying on with that smitten young doctor. Quick on that pedal" she suddenly demanded as she spied the chap from the electric company, who had been responsible for having her supply cut off, working on an electric pole from a precariously balanced high ladder.

With a nifty turn of the wheel Nitsa managed to topple the ladder, leaving the man from the electric company dangling dangerously from the pole. The two elderly ladies drove away cackling manically at what for them was an impossibly high speed of ten kilometres an hour.

Chapter 4: Bald Yannis Monetises His Goat

Quentin and Deirdre left Hattie lying down recuperating from the trauma of the hazardous mountainous drive and took a stroll around the village to reacquaint themselves with the sights. They exchanged pleasantries with Evangelia from the beauty parlour and waved at Tall Thomas as he drove by in his mobile refrigerated fish van.

"That's dried out nicely" Quentin commented, thinking the van looked in passable shape considering it had survived two soakings through sea submerges.

"It is so good to be back in Greece, it really is beginning to feel like home" Quentin mused, admiring the scenic beauty of the village.

"It is indeed. The village is just as I remember, but a tad hotter" Deirdre agreed, desperately fanning herself with Quentin's quaint Greek fisherman's hat.

Passing the hardware shop they were surprised to see a life-size cardboard cut-out of a goat dressed in a knitted two-piece pink number, comprising a little jacket and skirt. A sign invited customers to have their photo taken with the real goat for a bargain price of just two Euros. It also warned cameras and phones would be confiscated if people were caught in the act of taking illicit photos without the express permission of the goat's owner and without paying the quoted fee.

"Only Bald Yannis would think up a scheming way to monetise his pet" Deirdre said.

"Oh I don't know, I wouldn't be surprised if the odious Pappas hasn't got in on the act as well" Quentin quipped. "I wonder if Bald Yannis is finding it quite lucrative."

Bald Yannis was indeed hoping his scheme to monetise his darling pet goat Agapimeni would be extremely lucrative. He had been inspired by the recent arrival of two Japanese tourists in the village. After being separated during a mishap from the rest of their tour party they ended up on the wrong bus and arrived in Astakos looking very lost since the village did not feature in any of their copious notes of 'must-see things to photograph in Greece'.

Their equanimity was somewhat restored following a frantic phone conversation with their tour guide who promised them they would be rescued from the backwater village in a matter of hours and in the meantime they should make the best of this unprecedented situation by trying to amuse themselves without a guide list. The Japanese couple wandered around the village with perplexed looks, snapping pictures of Prosperous Pedros' fishing boat, Stavroula's taverna cat Boukali basking in the sunshine and a scowling Pappas.

They turned positively giddy at the sight of a burly bald man with a glaringly obvious and bad wispy hair transplant walking along the harbour front, dragging a goat kitted out in a pink knitted dress by a matching ribbon lead. Their cameras went into overdrive, attracting the attention of Bald Yannis who angrily denounced the invasion of his beloved pet goat's privacy. The Japanese couple were immediately abjectly apologetic for what they perceived as some awful cultural oversight; desperately trying to explain to Bald Yannis the sight of a goat wearing clothes was a novel phenomenon they had never experienced before.

Whipping out his wallet the Japanese gentleman offered to part with some cash to appease the irate Greek man and to pay for the unique opportunity of photographing his beautifully dressed goat. Never one to turn down the chance to earn some cash Bald Yannis agreed to let the couple pose with his pet goat, and for an additional sum he was even persuaded to pose with his darling goat too.

It was only several weeks later Bald Yannis discovered Agapimeni had become an Internet sensation on social media in Japan and had inspired a new wave of tourism which was about to hit the village. Thousands of Japanese tourists were planning to include Astakos in their foreign travel itineraries in a desperate quest to photograph his dressed up goat. Bald Yannis lost no time in commissioning a life sized cardboard cut-out of his goat so he would be ready to fully monetise this bizarre business opportunity.

With the arrival of the Japanese tourists imminent, Bald Yannis rushed over to the supermarket to ensure Mrs Kolokotronis was making speedy progress with her line of knitted goats' clothes.

Chapter 5: Catfished

Quentin and Deirdre joined Adonis for coffee in Stavroula's taverna where they regaled him with the tale of Hattie's unfortunate experience as the victim of a conniving catfish. She had fallen for the scam of a seemingly handsome man claiming to be English, professing his love for her from distant African parts where he said he had been sent on a secret and dangerous mission by his government. Hattie was oblivious to Quentin and Deirdre's concerns that the English grammar used by this supposedly English man was butchered far worse than that of their Greek friends,

"Randolph loved me, I inspired him to write poetry" Hattie insisted.

"Mother I keep telling you he copied that poetry from the middle of Hallmark greetings cards."

Every time Hattie's relatives tried to explain Randolph did not exist beyond his personae as a fraudster Hattie would cry "Of course he exists, I have seen his photograph. He wants to marry me as this engagement ring proves?"

"Mother you paid for the ring yourself and you have never even met this malaka" Quentin shouted, falling into typical Greek profanity. "You are being conned and you must stop sending money to this man."

"But he only needs another few thousand dollars to bribe his way out of that hell hole of an African jail and then he will be on the next plane to Idaho" Hattie claimed, unconvinced the new love of her life was anything but the genuine article.

"Mother, this month it is the jail you need to bail him out of, last month you sent him money for his emergency life-saving surgery and before that you paid for his extended hotel stay as the country was supposedly quarantined with that non-existent Ebola scare. You must accept you are being scammed and the photograph you are drooling over is an old picture of Roger Moore taken from a knitting pattern" Quentin proclaimed.

Hattie took no notice at all, telling her relatives "you just see me as old and cannot imagine I can still attract the attention of a slightly younger Englishman. I tell you Randolph loves me."

With that Quentin had marched his deluded mother into her bank and insisted on taking charge of her dwindling accounts. When the money failed to arrive to bail Randolph out of his African hell hole jail cell his letters had become more pleading and his phone calls more desperate. He had an inkling the money supply of this gullible old woman was about to dry up.

Fortunately Quentin had intercepted one of Randolph's phone calls. After telling the supposedly English 'catfisher', who spoke in a markedly pronounced foreign accent, he must be a remarkably privileged prisoner to be allowed so many phone calls from his hellish prison cell, Quentin went on to reveal he was on to his scam and would be informing the Nigerian police forthwith.

The letters and phone calls ceased instantly, leaving Hattie quite bereft as she was forced to cancel her planned engagement party. She missed the sweet nothings Randolph had shouted down the phone line at full volume as the scammer hadn't thought it a good idea to remind her to put her hearing aid in. She had reluctantly agreed to travel to Greece with her son and his wife in an effort to mend her broken heart. The most convincing argument Quentin had used to persuade his mother to venture to Greece was the agreeable company she would be sure to enjoy as there were two charming old ladies living in the house next door to his newly purchased 'Lemoni Spiti.'

Having heard this sorry tale Adonis immediately agreed Hattie needed a change of scenery. He promised he would by hook or by crook locate the missing borrowed builder and get him to work restoring the house so Quentin's aged mother could enjoy the company of her next door neighbours. He had only met Hattie briefly, but had sensed she was a difficult woman and seemingly immune to his charms, and would get on like a house on fire with the ghastly Fotini and Nitsa.

"Where on earth is Stavroula?" Deirdre questioned, noting they had been sat there for ages without any service.

Stavroula was standing in the kitchen covered in a layer of dust that had seeped into that night's specials. "'Ows I supposed to serve up dusty cookings?" she demanded to know, while swiping Slick Socrates round the head with a dusty pan lid. "Yous lawyer, do something lawyerly to get borrowed builder back ons job and finish off work."

The two of them stared in dismay at the half finished extension which was causing the dust emergency. Stavroula, using Slick Socrates money and a healthy injection of cash from her newly found father, that old fool Vasilis, had employed Achilles the borrowed builder to extend her taverna to incorporate a tourist tat shop. Stavroula had ambitions to rival Fat Christos' venture into the same type of tat he was selling at the inherited supermarket. However Achilles the borrowed builder's sudden disappearance had put a spanner in the works, leaving the intended shop space only half renovated and a thick coating of builders dust not only all over her taverna kitchen but also in all the pans of food.

Slick Socrates had flatly refused to don a pair of overalls and get on with a 'do-it-yourself' building job as he considered manual labour beneath him, claiming it could possibly mar the perfection of the single elongated fingernail he had proudly nurtured to an unnatural length. He also refused to inject any more cash into the project, convinced Achilles was an honest man who would turn up at some point with his pre-paid lump sum still safely in his bank account. Vasilis was willing to sink more cash into the project but he had to contend with mail order Masha's vociferous objections. She was demanding he use the money to satisfy her latest demand of fillers to emphasise her cheekbones as she was truly hooked on her addiction to plastic surgery.

"You aves customers" Socrates pointed out to Stavroula, eager to extricate himself from the awkward situation of Stavroula's relentless demands for more cash. He was beginning to get a sense of what his beloved had put her first two husbands through with her endless nagging.

Stavroula almost managed a genuine smile at the sight of the two Americans seated once again in her taverna. "K-Went-In and Did-Rees, goodly see yous" she declared, whilst wiping a thick layer of dust from her hair with her pinny. "Socrate bring wet cloths" she screeched, noticing the dust from her hair had fallen all over the table. At least the tablecloth was a wipe down waterproof one she reminded herself, admiring the lobster adorned shower curtain.

Adonis explained to Quentin and Deirdre, Stavroula had also been let down by Achilles the borrowed builder. It took some wily negotiating on his part to get all parties to agree if Achilles could be located he would have to split his day between the two jobs. "Yous won't gets tat shop open this tourist season anyways as is nearly over" he said convincingly to Stavroula "and this pair 'as aged mother with 'em and need 'ouse to live in."

"But malaka Achilles might not turn up" Stavroula cried "thens all money is lost." Adonis and Socrates insisted Achilles the borrowed builder was an honourable man and would reappear, having both known him for many years.

Unconvinced Stavroula stomped off to her kitchen where she didn't bother to remove the thick layer of dust lying like scum in the three coffees before serving them up.

Chapter 6: Achilles Suffers Amnesia

Achilles the borrowed builder was at that very moment on a faraway dirt track. It was one he had followed over the Albanian border back into Greece. He was now attempting to thumb a lift back to the village of Astakos. His pockets were empty and his recurring bouts of amnesia were still causing violent headaches.

He could not recall exactly how long he had been tied up in an Albanian barn in the middle of nowhere with shotguns pointed menacingly at him whenever he expressed his desire to leave. The only thing he was sure of was the whole horrible experience had put him off love.

At the start of the tourist season Achilles had so much work lined up he was considering borrowing another builder to expand his building business. A chance encounter with the beautiful Blerta had diverted his attention from his ambitions when he found himself smitten and, to his amazement, discovered his smitten feelings were reciprocated.

Blerta came from an exceptionally strict Albanian family living temporarily in Greece in search of extra work. Her family were horrified to discover her liaison with a Greek builder as they had promised her hand to a man in a neighbouring clan back in the homeland and poor Blerta had no say in the matter.

The romance between Achilles and Blerta had barely had chance to blossom when her family whisked her back home against her will. Achilles' mistake was in following his heart and tearing off to the remote dangerous reaches of northern Albania to rescue his beloved. Unfortunately for him his arrival resulted in utter disaster. As soon as he was spotted by Blerta's over protective relatives he was violently assaulted round the head with a shovel, resulting in amnesia, and thrown into a barn where he woke to find himself tied up and shackled by a long rusty chain around one ankle, with scuttling rats his only companions.

Every morning the barn door was pushed open a fraction and a bowl of unappetising swill left for him to devour. His captors appeared to favour a diet of 'pace', an Albanian speciality of boiled sheep's head flavoured with garlic and vinegar. The daily bottle of beer accompanying the rancid stew made Achilles long for a long glass of water.

Achilles was only released from his primitive captivity after several months when Blerta was safely married off to her family's chosen suitor. Achilles was sent on his way with a kick in the breeches and ominously warned terrible things would happen to him should he ever return. His temporary amnesia had wiped his memory clean of the strong emotions compelling him to pursue Blerta over the border and he cursed his stupidity in following the feelings of his heart he could no longer remember with any clarity.

All he wanted now was to get quickly back to Astakos as he sensed he had let people down who were relying on his building skills. It had already taken him days to tramp as far as the border, but safely back in Greece he hoped his arrival in Astakos would be quick.

Achilles sighed in relief when his thumb attracted the attention of a van transporting goats travelling in his direction, driven by a cheery Greek who was glad of his company.

"Looks likes yous 'ad a lucky escape to get out of that there Albanian clan village alive" the driver said when he'd heard as much as Achilles could remember of his ordeal. It wasn't the first time the goat driver had heard such tales on his travels and he felt much sympathy for his passenger with the bloodied and bandaged head. "'Ave a goat sandwich an' an aspirin" he offered "'an I'll 'ave you 'ome in Astakos befores you knows it."

Chapter 7: The Patter of Tiny Feet

The kafenion was all abuzz with the latest rumours on the gossip vine which the regulars were more than happy to exaggerate and spread indiscriminately. Unverified hearsay had it that old fool Vasilis was expecting the patter of tiny feet.

"Po po that old fool Vasilis is far too ancient to be a new father" Petros the Postman opined.

"Doesn't stop 'im 'avin regular prescriptions of Viagra" Vangelis the chemist interjected, blatantly ignoring patient confidentiality.

"'Appens that smitten young doctor 'as got mail order Masha pregnant" Bald Yannis mused.

"Might be a bit difficult as that old fool Vasilis bribed the 'ospital administrator to send smitten young doctor off to work in island clinic" Moronic Mitsos piped up.

"Well he might 'ave been sent off but he's still been sniffing round Masha on his visits back to mainland" Vangelis the chemist declared standing up to leave, feeling a pressing need to spread this piece of juicy gossip over the road in Stavroula's taverna.

That old fool Vasilis flew into a rage when he heard on the gossip vine that mail order Masha was pregnant, as she hadn't bothered to tell him. Considering he hadn't managed marital relations with Masha lately despite the copious amounts of Viagra his wife force fed him, he immediately jumped to the conclusion he had been cuckolded by the smitten young doctor. He was undecided whether to rush home to demand a divorce from his silicone wife or shoot the smitten young doctor first.

Stavroula too flew into a rage when she heard the gossip from Vangelis the chemist that her step-mother was pregnant. She presumed her prospective inheritance would be halved when that old fool Vasilis kicked the bucket and considered it unseemly that her newly found father would become a laughing stock by pushing a pram at his advanced age. Picking up the telephone she demanded Slick Socrates return home from his lawyerly office to discuss the matter with him.

"Ow many times I tells yous not to listen to gossip vine" Slick Socrates scolded when Stavroula told him she had heard that old fool Vasilis was expecting the patter of tiny feet. "It not Masha that pregnant but Vasilis' donkey that is expecting. Sotiris' donkey got Vasilis' donkey Onos pregnant and now the two old fools are taking my legal advice over who owns how much of soon to be born foal. Those two old fools will fight over anything and each is now claiming rights to be proud father of prospective donkey."

Stavroula pondered this information, asking Socrates "yous sure is no truth to rumours mail order Masha is pregnant?"

"I thinks if Vasilis so full of fatherly pride over Onos' potential offspring he woulds not 'ave kept quiet 'bout actual baby" Slick Socrates reassured his beloved, keeping a wary eye on the large frying pan she was brandishing in his direction.

Meanwhile that old fool Vasilis had returned home to confront his wife.

"Make a laughing stock of me woulds you, cuckolded 'usband last one to find out 'is wifes pregnant most likely from carryings on with smitten young doctor" Vasilis screeched as he crept up on Masha enjoying a spot of topless sunbathing in the garden.

"Who is pregnant?" Masha demanded to know.

"Don't tries to deny it, I 'eards it in village that you is 'aving baby" Vasilis insisted stridently.

"Wells it must be virgin birth then as you 'aven't managed to perform in ages" Masha mocked. "I not pregnant you fool, do you really think I would be drinking vodka if in family way? An' whats this nonsense about doctor, yous think I unfaithful to you?" she screamed while hurling the empty vodka bottle at him.

"Yous really not 'aving baby?" Vasilis questioned, beginning to realise he may have made a bit of an ass of himself by jumping to conclusions simply by listening to unsubstantiated village gossip.

Mail order Masha didn't deign to reply, simply shooting a withering look in the direction of her husband as she stomped into the house to pack her suitcases yet again.

Vasilis picked up the bottle Masha had thrown at him, hitting himself over the head with it as he cursed his stupidity. Then he rushed into the house to attempt to placate Masha with the promise of more plastic surgery and anything her heart desired from the jewellery shop.

Chapter 8: Business Booming Goodly

Following their scummy coffee at Stavroula's taverna Quentin and Deirdre urgently headed to the supermarket to buy some mouthwash. They waved at the man from the electricity company dangling precariously from the pole, mistaking his frantic waving for a pleasant greeting. Quentin strode straight past his former jogging partner without a glimmer of recognition since Fat Christos was almost unidentifiable as his former obese self following his rigorous dieting, stomach stapling surgery and his painful excess skin removal surgery. Fat Christos hailed his foreign friend with a forceful embrace, leading Quentin to believe a strange Greek man was propositioning him by the cheese counter.

"Yous no knows me K-Went-In?" Fat Christos questioned "I thinks I looks much better since you last saw me months ago, no?"

Recognising the voice of his friend, Quentin took a long hard look at the now slim man dressed in a sharp business suit and tie beneath a grubby apron. He returned the embrace with delight, telling Fat Christos his transformation was most remarkable. Tassia waddled out from behind the cheese counter, seemingly having gained as much weight as her husband had lost in her final months of pregnancy.

Perched on a stool behind the cash register Mrs Kolokotronis muttered "malaka" as she dropped a stitch, waving her needles at the Americans to indicate she had to get on with her knitting. Her unique line of fisherman's pullovers was proving a roaring success in the supermarket, in addition to meeting Bald Yannis' constant requests for innovative goat's clothes. Her expertise with the knitting needles left her in constant demand, so much so she had signed up Thea as an apprentice. Thea had enthusiastically taken on the work as it helped her make enough money to keep the debt collectors at bay and she knitted as she watched her favourite soap operas.

"Good grief you have really expanded your line of tourist tat" Deirdre declared to Fat Christos, surveying shelves heaving under the weight of glow in the dark Parthenon's, evil eye earrings, key rings and Christmas tree ornaments, Greek flag dog collars, worry beads, wind-up Greek dancing dolls and breakable wedding plates.

"Naked statues most popular but I keeps 'em on top shelf away from Mama to stops 'er wrapping 'em up in brown paper" Fat Christos said, explaining his mother could be a puritanical prude.

"Business booming goodly" Fat Christos replied in response to Quentin's question about how things were going "an' we maybe come neighbours as we plans to turn Tassia's old dead uncles 'ouse into a holiday home for whens we needs break."

"But surely that house is only just down the road in Rapanaki so you won't really be getting away from things" Quentin queried.

"You can says that but yous don't live with my mother" Fat Christos said, whispering Mrs Kolokotronis had moved in with him and Tassia over the summer and was proving to be a most interfering old bat. Quentin sympathised, confiding to Fat Christos his own very difficult mother was accompanying him and Deirdre on this trip.

"Well send 'er to me if she's a dab hand at knitting" Mrs Kolokotronis commanded, fearing she would fall behind with all her knitted commissions unless she could rake in some extra help.

Fat Christos promised to join Quentin and Deirdre in the taverna that evening to catch up on all the local gossip.

Stepping outside, the pair were just in time to witness the agonised fall of the man from the electric company. He lost his precarious hold on the electric pole, from which he had been dangling for a good half-hour, to the complete amusement of Bald Yannis who had watched Nitsa's deliberate hit and run of the ladder but done nothing to assist the dangling man. The electricity company employee landed on the ground with a nasty splat and the air reverberated with the sound of his screams and the shattering of his bones.

"Call an ambulance" Quentin shouted to Fat Christos over the raucous laughter of Bald Yannis who stood in the hardware shop doorway spluttering "I wondered how long he could 'old on."

Chapter 9: Hattie Flags Down A Taxi

Whilst Quentin and Deirdre were wandering around the village Hattie was taking advantage of the quiet time alone to brush up on her Greek. Ever since her son and his wife suggested she accompany them on their trip to this foreign land she had been toiling with the task of getting to grips with the complexity of the Greek language as a way of taking her mind off her broken heart and her obsession with Randolph. She planned to surprise her son with her linguistic skills as he had no idea she had been studying most assiduously. Her mastery of the difficult language would show him once and for all that she still retained all the marbles he accused her of losing over Randolph.

She was annoyed the house Quentin had raved about so much had turned out to be a dilapidated ruin as she didn't like being cooped up in Yiota's room over the taverna, even though the balcony provided a beautiful view of the sea and the harbour. Now it was time to put her new language skills to practical use and Hattie decided to take a turn around the village. After anointing every exposed inch of her body in vinegar as a precaution against blood sucking mosquitoes she ventured outdoors smelling like a chip shop and was just in time to flag down a passing taxi.

As the old Mercedes taxi took a very slow turn around the village Hattie was delighted to discover her Greek words were understood by the driver and her companion. It was her first time actually attempting to communicate and she ensured she enunciated each syllable very slowly and loudly.

Pancratius the village policeman pulled the taxi over, accusing Nitsa, the driver, of causing injuries to the man from the electric company by deliberately driving into his ladder half-an-hour earlier. "Impossible" interjected Hattie from the back seat in a commanding tone of mutilated Greek, "the hour minus one half I am in this taxi not near here as employ at airport."

"But I have a goodly description it was indeed Nitsa's taxi knocked electric man off ladder" insisted the easily confused policeman.

Nitsa caught on to the alibi her new passenger was helpfully providing and insisted her taxi had only just arrived in the village from the airport, thus she could not possibly be the guilty party. Hattie interrupted once again, insisting in excruciating ear-piercing Greek "I employ taxi as chauffeur and now police car make me 'siga siga.'"

Pancratius, not totally convinced of Nitsa's innocence, reluctantly allowed her to drive on after once again reminding her she must acquire a legal taxi licence to pick up paying passengers. Hattie yet again butted in, telling the policeman she was not a paying passenger but an American citizen.

The three old ladies burst into cackling laughter as soon as they drove out of sight of the policeman. Nitsa thanked Hattie for the ready lies she had come up with as an alibi. Introducing herself and Fotini she insisted on Hattie joining them for a drink to celebrate getting one over on the dunderheaded policeman.

The introductions revealed Hattie should have been their new neighbour and they commiserated on her being stuck in a room over Yiota's taverna rather than enjoying a house with a garden. As the two old crones were all too familiar with their own son's disdain and barely concealed contempt for their ways, they were totally sympathetic to Hattie's tale of being trapped under the watchful eye of Quentin. By the time the threesome had knocked back several glasses of brandy each at a little taverna in Marouli it was decided Hattie would move in with her new found friends until renovations at the 'Lemoni Spiti' were completed.

"We best drives back carefully to get your luggage" Nitsa said "as we dont's want to draw attention of Pancratius with 'is breathalyser."

Chapter 10: Quivering Quentin

By the time Quentin and Deirdre entered 'Mono Ellinika Trofima' they were in a state of quivering panic. The pleasant evening they had envisaged spending catching up with the company of their dear Greek friends had been ruined by the disappearance of Hattie, which they had discovered when they knocked on her door to tell her it was time for dinner. The room was empty and all her luggage had gone, leading Quentin and Deirdre to the alarming conclusion Hattie had been abducted.

Ignoring the courteous formalities they should have exchanged with the locals after their months long absence the American pair burst into the taverna, declaring the police must be contacted as a matter of urgency. As they explained the plight of their missing mother Prosperous Pedros leapt up to reassure them Hattie was safely ensconced in the house of his own mother Fotini, and planned to stay with the two old crones until the 'Lemoni Spiti' was habitable.

Quentin was confounded by this news, wondering how on earth his mother was able to communicate with their Rapanaki neighbours enough to move in with them.

"She speaking some kind of mangled confused Greek my mother can unravel" Prosperous Pedros explained.

"Perhaps it is some common old crone speak" Gorgeous Yiorgos volunteered, before Yiota jumped to Hattie's defence, declaring

"Hattie has been learning Greek from books and demonstrates remarkable dexterity in her grasp of a new language at her advanced age. I expect she could give you lessons K-Went-In as your own mastery of Greek leaves a lot to be desired."

"I am shocked. I had no idea my mother was studying the language" Quentin said.

"That's the trouble with you youngsters" Sotiris, the

ancient neighbour and sparring partner of that old fool Vasilis butted in, "you never pay attention to what us oldies do, too busy wrapped up in your own concerns to take an interest in our affairs."

"I have been very concerned about my mother's atrocious affair with her fake fiancé and brought her out here so she would forget her broken heart" Quentin declared, hurt to the quick people would assume he gave no thought to his mother.

"Oh well she seemed 'appy enough settled with my mother and cousin Nitsa" Prosperous Pedros reassured him, adding "the best way to mend her broken heart is to let her enjoy the company of like- minded ladies of her own age. My mother is less demanding of me since Nitsa moved in and she rarely asks when my dead father is returning from Athens anymore."

Prosperous Pedros had a valid point but Quentin still had to have the last word, insisting "it was still very thoughtless of mother to move in with Fotini and Nitsa without even bothering to tell me."

"Sit down and order some food to take yous minds off it" Takis advised, recommending they try Yiota's soupia soup. Quentin and Deirdre were totally baffled by the idea of soupy soup, thinking it sounded suspiciously soapy, until Prosperous Pedros explained soupia was the Greek word for cuttlefish.

The locals were eager to acquaint Quentin and Deirdre with all the local gossip. The Orthodox Church had sent the Pappas on a refresher course, believing he needed to brush up on his priestly duties. The Pappas had only grudgingly agreed to attend the refresher course when his higher-ups had threatened him with excommunication if he didn't show up. He had been banned from selling cutlery from his briefcase and warned if Petula appeared with any more bruises he would be sent to serve a penance in a monastery.

Since his return to Astakos the Pappas remarkably appeared to have changed his ways and was sober at all times. He had developed heady ambitions of progressing up the church job ladder, attracted by the higher wages and more flattering robes.

Tall Thomas seemed rather despondent as his mobile refrigerated fish van business was being threatened by a rival fish selling business, based in Gavros, encroaching on his established territory. Forced to lower his prices due to this mobile competition he conceded the only way to keep his own business viable was to come up with a cunning plan to nobble the competition.

Suddenly all the fishermen stopped slouching, pulling themselves into upright positions and sucking their stomachs in as mail order Masha made a dramatic entrance in a dress so skin tight it would have been impossible to conceal any baby bump. That old fool Vasilis followed her in a dejected fashion, regretting his folly in falling for the outrageous lies spread by the village gossip vine that had just cost him a small fortune in the jewellery shop.

"Yous all 'orrible gossips" mail order Masha accused the room at large "and shoulds be ashamed of yourselves for saying I is pregnant when I is not. Yous not know heartbreak of wanting baby and being stuck with old fool what is past it."

The villagers failed to meet her eye, staring at the floor and willing it to open up and swallow them. Everyone there was guilty of gossip, but it was rare that anyone openly denounced the ubiquitous practice.

Deirdre broke the heavily laden silence by rushing over to hug mail order Masha, telling her how much she was looking forward to tasting her infamous borscht. She could not fail to admire the brilliance of the ostentatious egg-sized ring adorning Masha's finger, bringing a satisfied smile to Masha's face.

"My 'usband love me so much he insist on buying bigliest diamond in shop" Masha declared, not mentioning that his guilt offering was the only thing that prevented her packing up her suitcases and leaving him. She had given the old fool several ultimatums, declaring if he ever again accused her of cheating she would leave and take his precious donkey with her, and demanding he increase his intake of Viagra and give her a baby.

Masha turned her nose up at the suggestion of soupia soup, stating any other soup was inferior to her superior borscht. Fluttering her eyelashes at Tall Thomas she told him she would appreciate it if he could get some lobster for Yiota to cook as it was the most expensive dish she could imagine and she intended to make that old fool Vasilis continue to pay for his suspicious thoughts. Tucking into a generous plate of fried kalamari she mused her now deflated husband would not dare accuse her of anything, thus leaving the door open for her to resume her clandestine meetings with the smitten young doctor whenever she could entice him back to the mainland.

The atmosphere lightened, the wine flowed and everyone enjoyed Yiota's delicious home cooked dishes. A dramatic second silence followed as the taverna door opened and Achilles the borrowed builder entered, eliciting gasps of astonishment at his sudden return with his grubbily bandaged head. His recent horrendous ordeal, coupled with his still partial amnesia and the stress of the long journey home, had left him confused. Spying the familiar figure of Adonis he sank to his knees in relief and began to recount what he could remember of the events of the last several months.

Adonis caught Quentin's eye and mouthed over the prostrate figure of the borrowed builder that everything would now be all right and work on the 'Lemoni Spiti' would resume the next morning.

Chapter 11: Toothless Tasos' Exorbitant Electric Bill

Toothless Tasos' life had changed drastically since the goddess of his dreams, Thea, had moved in with him. His house had been transformed into a home with the addition of Thea's homely womanly touches and he no longer spent all his waking hours dreaming of her. Returning home from fishing he approached the house with equal measures of anticipation and apprehension. Much as he was delighted to know Thea would most likely be waiting for him he never quite knew what new changes awaited.

Thea was able to keep her debt woes at arm's length by using the rental income from her harbour-side house and the wages from her knitting job to keep up the strict monthly payment regime imposed by the debt collection agency employed by the home shopping channel. Toothless Tasos provided all their day-to-day living expenses and endeavoured to keep a lid on Thea's spendthrift ways.

After selling his catch of the day to Tall Thomas to hawk from his mobile refrigerated fish van, Toothless Tasos was strolling home, looking forward to a morning cup of coffee prepared by the fair hands of his beloved goddess. In seconds his good mood evaporated to be replaced with apoplectic rage when Petros the Postman handed over the latest electricity bill. The stated sum was astronomical. Toothless Tasos presumed it was a grossly overestimated estimated bill and rushed to the outdoor electric meter, only to confirm the electricity used did indeed relate to the numbers in the humongous bill he was clutching in his now clammy hands.

As he let himself into the house he was saddened to discover Thea was not home. Sinking despondently into the deckchair in the living room he mulled over the possible reasons his electricity consumption had soared so monstrously. How could two people living together account for such a huge surge in extra electricity usage since it had been very hot and no heating appliances had been needed? Although Thea had constantly nagged him to install air-conditioning he had resisted on the grounds it was a needlessly expensive luxury. He was at a complete loss to explain away the massive rise in electricity usage and decided to telephone the electric company and demand they send a man round to investigate.

The usual man employed by the electricity company in Astakos was unfortunately lying in a hospital bed, encased from head to toe in plaster with his broken legs raised by a winch, following his painful fall from the electricity pole when Nitsa had deliberately knocked over his ladder with her old Mercedes taxi. The electricity company promised to send someone over quickly and Toothless Tasos assured them someone would be at home to receive him.

Thea's knitting was lying neglected on top of the fridge and Toothless Tasos wondered where his beloved could be when she had urgent knitting piling up. He always felt a pang of disappointment if Thea was not home to greet him as it reminded him of all the lonely years before she moved in. Once again he pondered on the possible ways he could persuade Thea to share his bedroom. She insisted they could not indulge in romantic marital relations until they were actually married as she had her good reputation to retain. This left him permanently frustrated.

The situation of his marriage to Stavroula remained unresolved despite countless visits to seek lawerly advice from Slick Socrates. Momentarily forgetting his anger over the exorbitant electricity bill Toothless Tasos resolved to make more of a romantic effort with Thea in a bid to win his wicked way into her bedroom. He would take a walk up to the graveyard and see if he could pick up some free flowers for her.

Luckily for Toothless Tasos the Pappas was not hanging around the church or the graveyard. He was visiting Mrs Christeas, a widowed parishioner who had recently moved into Thea's harbour-side house. She appeared to be an exemplary tenant and a good Christian woman who spent many hours attending his church services. The Pappas could not help compare this handsome woman, a mere ten years his senior, to his own downtrodden wife Petula. He considered Mrs Christeas a woman of impeccable taste, with exceptional book learning for a member of the fairer sex. He was flattered by the more than churchly interest she showed in him and contemplated with a fine woman like Mrs Christeas by his side he could have achieved far more in life than he had up to now with his peasant-minded wife.

Mrs Christeas was encouraging him to set his sights on a higher church role than the one he currently held and her constant flattery was going to his head. As he was taking his leave from her to return to the church she uttered a bold and forward statement, saying "*fere ladi kai ela vradi.*"

The Pappas was taken by surprise by this invitation to bring olive oil in the evening, this being a traditional sign of courtship. He had never been courted in his life and his head swelled enormously with the implications of the invitation. What excuse could he give to his wife Petula to explain his absence that evening and where could he find some cheap olive oil? His own supply was almost gone and Petula rigorously rationed the small quantity left. Recollecting the church font was still full of olive oil from the latest baptism he cheered up, realising he could siphon some of it off into a bottle and present it to the widow Christeas that very evening.

The Pappas had a busy afternoon planned organising a protest against the new nudist beach which had inadvertently sprung up on the village outskirts. Much as he secretly enjoyed the sights of naked tourist women flaunting their bodies, hypocritically he knew it would go down very well with his superiors if he denounced such immorality. He had signatures to collect for the petition and his stance against the nudist beach was most definitely improving his own standing with the ladies of Astakos.

Whilst the Pappas had been lapping up the undisguised admiration of another woman, his wife Petula was at home giving his pet goat Nero a bubble bath. Although it was months now since the Pappas had been free with his fists she was still desperately unhappy, trapped in the loveless marriage. It saddened her to see Gorgeous Yiorgos bestow all his attention on the tourist women over the summer, though she had no idea his heart was not really in the art of kamaki any more and he still harboured fond feelings for Petula. Now her husband was sober and non-violent she had no solid grounds for a divorce which could ruin his reputation. The only affection in her life came from Nero the pet goat and she presumed even if she extricated herself from the marriage the Pappas would claim custody of the goat.

Gorgeous Yiorgos really had lost interest in making kamaki to loose foreign tourist women and only kept up the practice out of habit. He admitted to himself he had lost his heart to Petula, but she had made the decision to stay with her husband out of a misguided sense of loyalty. He still gave her driving lessons and dreaded the day when she would pass the test. He kept a watchful eye on the Pappas, feeling sooner or later he would trip himself up and give Petula a good reason to consider leaving. He wasn't taken in by the Pappas' sober ways and his fake God-bothering.

Toothless Tasos rushed home from the graveyard with his posy of graveside purloined flowers as he had received a telephone call from the electricity company to say a man had been dispatched to make the necessary checks. Stepping into the house he walked straight into the middle of a furious row between Thea and an official looking man with a clipboard.

"'Ow else I supposed to stay cool when tight wad Toothless Tasos won't let me 'ave air-conditioning" Thea screamed.

"What's going on?" Toothless Tasos demanded, only to be told by the man from the electricity company the exorbitant electric usage was down to Thea sitting next to the open fridge door all day knitting.

"It only cold air in 'ouse" she proclaimed in defence of her chosen spot. "Mrs Kolokotronis nots want knitting I 'ave sweated all over."

Toothless Tasos put his head in his hands as he reluctantly scolded Thea for her stupidity. "You cants sit with fridge door opens all day woman, it costs a fortune." Remembering his resolution to be more romantic he added "I sorry to be cross my cherub, I says no more about it if you keep fridge door shut in future. 'Ave these flowers and I goes to hardware shops to buys you fan."

Chapter 12: Watch Your Fingers In The Fan

"Where's that gorgeous goat of yours today Yanni?" Toothless Tasos asked Bald Yannnis as he walked into the hardware shop.

"If you mean Agapemini" Bald Yannis replied, "she is having a break in Moronic Mitsos' overgrown garden as he does not want to spend his generous police pension on hiring someone to do his weeding, 'an goat is cheaper."

"He paying yous for use of goat then?" Toothless Tasos enquired.

"Of course he pays, Mitsos is a moron" Bald Yannis laughed, demonstrating no shame in belittling the intelligence of his only friend. "What's you want to buy Taso, I not got all day to stand around chatting?"

"I 'ave come for a fan to keep Thea cool as she 'as cost me a fortune by sitting all day with fridge door open."

"What a fool that woman is" Bald Yannis declared, staring Toothless Tasos down as though daring him to deny it.

Tasos insisted Bald Yannis plug in the fan to demonstrate its cooling capabilities. Flicking the switch to the 'on' position Bald Yannis advised "Tell Thea not to stick 'er fingers in it."

"Why what 'arm can this 'ere fan do to fingers?" Toothless Tasos questioned, while nonchalantly sticking his index finger between the rotating blades. "Malaka" he screamed as half his finger was sliced off and the severed digit flew across the hardware shop, landing in an open tin of dark green resilient boat paint.

"Who knew you were more stupid than woman you lives with?" Bald Yannis exclaimed, tossing an oily rag he used to clean the chainsaw at Tasos and telling him to use it to stop the flow of blood. "Dont's get blood all over my stock" he instructed, adding "I'll have to charge you for this paint now as blood from yous finger will turn it yellow."

"Fish it out" Toothless Tasos screamed "they mights be able to sew it backs on at 'ospital."

Reluctantly Bald Yannis stuck his hand in the paint pot and tossed the decapitated fingertip to Tasos who ran outside and flagged down a passing taxi to take him to the hospital. Bald Yannis followed in hot pursuit, waving his now green hand in the air and demanding his cash for the contaminated paint while reminding Tasos his shop did not extend credit. Tasos let loose a stream of expletives, causing Nitsa to turn round from the driving seat and whack him over the head with the stick she kept handy for threatening reluctant-to-pay passengers.

"I'll 'ave none of that bad language in my taxi young man and dont's gets blood on my upholstery" she declared haughtily. "Is yous coming to 'ospital too?" she asked Bald Yannis, hoping it would give her a chance to get up close and personal with him while demonstrating her charms.

"Not likely, I goes get money from Thea for paint and tells 'er Tasos at 'ospital" Bald Yannis replied, wondering if he could persuade Thea to purchase the fan if he removed the bloody scraps of skin from the blades first. "Best get Stavroula to pass you some ice for yous finger else it will be dead useless by times you get to 'ospital" he recommended.

Stavroula rushed over to the taxi with a plastic bag of ice cubes and grabbing the decapitated green finger tip from Tasos threw it inside. Instructing Slick Socrates to keep an eye on the taverna she jumped in the taxi to accompany her supposedly dead husband to the hospital. Relations between them had remained cordial since Toothless Tasos had prevented her demise at the strangling hands of the elusive underwear thief and she no longer wasted any time plotting his murder.

Mrs Christeas rubbed her hands in glee as she watched Stavroula depart in the taxi from the window of her rented harbour-side house. She was most delighted for this gave her a wonderful opportunity to source the necessary rooster needed as a vital ingredient in the evening meal she must prepare for the Pappas. Mrs Christeas liked to abide by the old village custom dictating a courting man bearing olive oil should be greeted with a home cooked meal of **Κόκορας κοκκινιστός με χυλοπίτες.** This tasty dish of rooster in red sauce with noodles must be cooked to perfection to win the approval of the courting suitor.

Mrs Christeas knew it would be hard to find a suitable rooster as shop bought ones were clearly a bit 'iffy' and far inferior to free range ones. An aged bird with long and strong bones was required and no one could be sure of the origins of a rooster purchased in a shop. She knew Stavroula had a most excellent aged rooster pecking around in her back garden. So intent in inveigling her way into the good graces of the Pappas she never considered cooking up Stavroula's prized rooster would be stealing. She thought of Stavroula as a bossy and obnoxious woman who never had the good grace to attend church and had no reservations about her planned act of theft.

Timing her poultry theft to coincide with the siesta hours when most villagers were catching forty winks, Mrs Christeas snuck into Stavroula's garden and surreptitiously stuffed the prize rooster inside an old olive sack with pilfering abandon. A quick twist of its neck was followed by a feverish bout of feather plucking and in no time at all the chopped up cock was boiling away in the cooking pot.

Bald Yannis was cursing his own stupidity for sticking his hand in the pot of green paint to retrieve Toothless Tasos' decapitated finger. The industrial strength boat paint was proving impossible to wash off even with the aid of copious amounts of turpentine. With hindsight he wished he had left the finger to rot and surmised he may have even got a better price for the paint if he had marketed it as having an 'added something extra'. Picking up the fan he strode over to Toothless Tasos' house and demanded Thea settle up the outstanding bill for the fan and the contaminated paint immediately. Once Thea located Toothless Tasos' secret stash of cash stufffed inside an old teapot and Bald Yannis safely secured the money on his person he dropped the bombshell that Toothless Tasos was at the hospital, hoping to have his fingertip sewn back on. "Whatever yous do Thea dont's stick any fingers in fan" he advised as he took his leave.

Thea immediately went indoors and turned the fan on, finding if she positioned it just right it created a nice cross breeze between the fan and the open fridge door. Taking up her knitting she enjoyed the selfish thought the house would be peaceful without Tasos hanging round and nagging her about her spendthrift habits. It never occurred to her the seemly thing to do would be to rush to her fiancés side at the hospital and comfort him over the trauma he had experienced.

Chapter 13: The Arrest Warrant

Quentin and Deirdre, accompanied by Adonis, were delighted to discover Achilles the borrowed builder hard at work renovating the 'Lemoni Spiti' on the morning after his return to Astakos. As Adonis and Slick Socrates had predicted, the balance of money already paid to Achilles was sitting safely in his bank account, affirming his reputation as an honest man. He had borrowed two strapping young builders to help with the work and they were busy making excellent progress on the kitchen. He was desperately apologetic for his prolonged absence but his clients were sympathetic to the ghastly plight he had endured at the hands of the Albanian mafia clan.

Slick Socrates had used all his charm to persuade Stavroula to let the builders make a head start on the 'Lemoni Spiti' rather than first beginning the expansion of her taverna into a tourist tat annex. He had pointed out the few remaining tourists would be put off by the dust and the banging. In exchange for his interference Adonis had bartered an agreement to let Socrates attend to any legal matters likely to arise in his hotel business.

Whilst the building work progressed Quentin climbed over the wall into Fotini's neighbouring garden, where he confronted his mother about her hasty departure from her room over Yiota's taverna. "Oh Quentin don't fuss so" Hattie said. "Fotini and Nitsa have welcomed me into their home and it is so nice to have the companionship of women my own age. I have a lovely garden to enjoy and I can keep a beady eye on your builders from here."

"Are you sure you are not intruding on Fotini's hospitality? She has a reputation for not being exactly welcoming to visitors" Quentin asked.

"She just doesn't tolerate fools" Hattie replied. "I hear when you were made welcome in her home you went blabbing all over the village about how she had papered her living room wall with bank notes, leading to an unfortunate break-in and an arson attack."

Quentin blanched at this statement as he had never previously made the connection between the break-in and his gossiping ways. "Will you at least join us for dinner in the taverna this evening?" he asked his mother, to which she replied,

"Another time Quentin, tonight I have promised to cook Idaho potato hash followed by Idaho potato ice cream. Fotini has had no chance to sample foreign foods and was thrilled to hear of the many amazing and tasty things I can do with potatoes."

Just then a police car drove up to Fotini's house and an officious looking policeman stepped out and hammered on the door. Fotini reluctantly opened the door, annoyed by the intrusion but not daring to lob lemons at him as she did with other unwanted visiting pests.

"I 'ave a warrant to arrest Kyria Nitsa" the policeman announced.

"Whys you heres instead of that numbskull Pancratius?" Fotini demanded to know.

"This is a serious matter requiring a more senior police officer with no local connections to the area" the policeman replied. "Kindly tell Kyria Nitsa to come outside to be handcuffed at once."

"She not 'ere, she gone for drive" Fotini retorted.

"No doubt causing havoc in her unlicensed illegal taxi" the policeman stated, wondering if he had any grounds to demand the two watching Americans produce their passports to prove they were not illegal immigrants. "I'll be back" he threatened as he left.

"Surely they can't arrest an old lady like Nitsa for simply driving round in her old Mercedes taxi" Hattie opined.

"Is more than illicit taxi" Adonis piped up. "I 'ears there

is witness to testify Nitsa deliberately knocked over electric man's ladder an' put 'im in 'ospital with serious injuries. Electric company not turn blind eye to that no matters how many brown envelopes Nitsa tries to bribe 'em with."

"But who would tell tales on cousin Nitsa?" Fotini asked.

"Well it 'as to be that 'orrid Bald Yannis as he saw whole incident" Adonis replied.

"Don't lets Nitsa know, she has soft spot for that bald malaka who she says as 'is eye on 'er. She will keenly sense 'is betrayal" Fotini cried.

Fotini's revelation of a possible sexual connection between Bald Yannis and the old crone left her audience completely repulsed as they tried to eliminate the awful images invading their minds.

Quentin turned a disappointed eye on his mother and asked her if she knew she was staying in the company of a wanted felon. Hattie blushed and hoped she would not be found out for making up an outright alibi lie to the local police, but quickly realised she could plead her use of mangled Greek had led to a misunderstanding if she was dragged into the police enquiry.

"Has mother got herself into another scrape?" Deirdre asked as she climbed over the garden wall to join her husband. She had been busy discussing the bizarre plumbing system Achilles the borrowed builder intended to install in the house. "I thought when we had our own house we would be able to flush things down the toilet, but Achilles tells me it can't be done and we will have to use one of those ghastly bins. We will need to put up a big sign to deter any visiting friends from America causing a blockage."

"Well at least we will have a patriotic shower curtain hanging up in the bathroom to take their minds of it" Quentin quipped.

Adonis took a call on his mobile phone and announced he must return to Astakos immediately as the first Japanese tourists had just arrived at his hotel and he wanted to be there to greet them. It could turn into an opportunity to make a commission from the sale of houses he knew some of the locals wanted off-loading to reduce their property tax liabilities. He presumed Japanese tourists would be as gullible and easily charmed as this pair of Americans had been, but had less than two weeks to try and make a sale. This limited time span would necessitate a charm overload.

As Quentin and Deirdre piled into Adonis' pick-up truck Hattie told Quentin to go to the supermarket and fetch her some potatoes, but with Nitsa's fate up in the air she wasn't sure how many people she would be cooking for that evening.

Chapter 14: Dandruff and Handcuffs

The Pappas was busy knocking loudly on doors in Astakos, deliberately ignoring the unwritten rule not to disturb people during the siesta hours. He was gathering as many signatures as he could for his petition to stop people stripping their clothes off on the local beach to prevent it becoming a haven for nudists. Thea was not at all happy to be dragged away from her favourite soap opera 'Seven Deadly Mothers-in-Law' to answer the door to the odious priest. Nevertheless she signed the petition as she did not think it appropriate children should be subjected to the sight of bare flesh while playing on the beach.

The Pappas expected Tasos to sign his petition too but Thea told him he would need to go to the hospital to find him. She was not sure if Tasos would be able to sign anything unless his finger was successfully sewn back on. She had a slight tinge of guilt over not rushing to the hospital, but convinced herself Tasos would not be happy if she splashed out on the exorbitant taxi fare.

That old fool Vasilis and mail order Masha were having no truck at all with the Pappas' petition. Masha hurled a mouthful of Russian expletives at the priest for interrupting their attempt to get pregnant and the married couple had never forgiven the Pappas' attempt to blackmail Vasilis. Their neighbour Sotiris openly scoffed at the Pappas' latest nonsense, pointing out "at my advanced years you woulds stop my only 'opes of ever catching sight of naked woman? Yous is deluded."

The Pappas had more luck at the supermarket as Mrs Kolokotronis, well known for her prudery, was happy to sign on her own behalf as well as adding Fat Christos' and Tassia's signatures. Bald Yannis conned the Pappas by signing the name of his goat Agapemini rather than his own.

"'Ow comes your dandruff is black? It looks really

nasty, 'ave you some 'ideous scalp disease?" the Pappas asked Bald Yannis, noticing clumps of a black power like substance smeared over Bald Yannis' bald pate, apparently emanating from his ridiculous botched transplanted hair.

Bald Yannis did not deign to reply as he rushed into Evangelia's beauty parlour to check out his scalp in her mirror. To his horror he discovered the expensive branded hair growth and thickening powder he had liberally applied to his head had smeared across his scalp and did indeed resemble black dandruff. Even worse it had coagulated into clammy clumps, accentuating the obvious circular scars still noticeably visible from his botched hair transplant.

"You told me this 'ere expensive branded hair powder would make my 'air thicker, not makes me look like moulting coal miner" Bald Yannis accused Evangelia, who had reluctantly sourced the hair restorative powder for this belligerent customer.

"I told yous I could gets it for yous but knows nothing about it beyond what it said on box" Evangelia said in her defence. "Did you apply it like what the instructions said?"

"I sprayed the muck on my 'ead, 'ow 'ard can it be?" Bald Yannis retorted, recalling he had in typical male fashion completely ignored the instruction pamphlet.

"Well I can shampoo it out" Evangelia offered, quoting her price for a shampoo and blow dry.

"Po po, I nots waste money on overpriced beauty treatments, I wash it off at 'ome with bar of soap" Bald Yannis retorted, slamming the door and leaving a trail of black powder in his wake. Ordering a coffee at the kafenion he settled down to eavesdrop the latest chatter. The gossip centred on Quentin's mother Hattie. No one could believe anyone would have been so naive and gullible as to send huge amounts of cash to a complete stranger they had never met who declared undying love on that new fangled internet.

This was the first Bald Yannis had heard of this 'catfish'

scam and he was immediately incensed he had never had the foresight to monetise his own dating scam, which he had run solely for his own amusement. He pondered if there was a way to make some money from his own scam and if Moronic Mitsos could be persuaded to send some of his generous police pension to a woman who only existed in Bald Yannis' imagination, redirecting any cash sent to his own bank account of course. He needed something to replace the fun he had derived from stealing underwear off the village washing lines.

The villagers taking coffee at the kafenion were suddenly shaken out of their gossiping by the sound of a siren approaching. Nitsa's old Mercedes taxi drove into sight at a speed they had never witnessed the slow taxi move at before, hotly pursued by a police car with sirens blaring. Nitsa only came to a reluctant halt as her passenger Stavroula, returning from the hospital, was insisting on being let out.

The senior police officer strolled from his car, demanding Nitsa get out of the taxi. Climbing down from the pile of old magazines she was balanced on to see out of the windscreen, Nitsa succumbed to the handcuffs and her very public arrest. As the senior police officer guided her into the back of his car Nitsa implored her kafenion audience to get her a lawyer and protest her unjustifiable arrest, screeching "I is innocent old woman, this police brutality, do somethings quick 'fore they throw me in a hellhole prison cell."

Chapter 15: Stavroula's Missing Rooster

Stavroula returned from the hospital in remarkable good cheer. Fortunately for Toothless Tasos the smitten young doctor had been reassigned from the islands to the local hospital and boasted he had the necessary skills to reattach the severed fingertip. He had lamentably overestimated his own capabilities in this most delicate surgical procedure. Although he had managed to successfully reattach the sliced off fingertip he had sewn it back the wrong way round, resulting in the finger nail now facing the palm. Thea had not bothered to rush to her fiancés side Stavroula noted, leaving her feeling smug. She knew beyond a shadow of a doubt if she ever ended up in hospital her darling Socrates would rush instantly to her side.

Feeling suddenly appreciative of Socrates made Stavroula decide to do something nice to show her affection for the man in her life. She decided as a special treat to cook up his favourite meal of rooster in red sauce with noodles, a dish she hadn't prepared since the night he first courted her with a bottle of olive oil. She would serve the rooster to him in her sexiest negligee as a prelude to seducing him. She had been saving her last rooster for a special occasion and decided now was the moment to wring its neck and start cooking.

Stepping into the garden Stavroula was perplexed to see no sign of the rooster. Sticking her head in the chicken coop revealed the rooster was not taking a siesta. After searching high and low Stavroula concluded the rooster had either escaped or been stolen. Not wanting to draw Socrates' attention to the meal she secretly planned she decided to take a stroll around the village to try and spot the missing rooster before announcing its absence.

Slick Socrates put a spoke in her plans when he said he could not mind the taverna any longer as Tall Thomas had requested he rush to the police station to represent his Aunty Nitsa who had been arrested for dangerously driving an unlicensed taxi and malicious bodily harm of an employee of the electric company. He explained these were serious charges and he must act urgently to prevent her being held in a cell overnight. Stavroula was only convinced Slick Socrates should represent Nitsa when she learnt of the large fee her lover would earn for his legal services.

"She is a menace on the roads though" Stavourla stated. "I 'ave just been in 'er taxi and she backed into an ambulance outside 'ospital, nearly giving me whiplash. Still I 'ad a good laugh when she drove over foot of smitten young doctor who is back and no doubt will be sniffing around step-mother again. He won't get so far now on 'is crutches."

Socrates dashed off on his mission to extricate Nitsa from police custody, leaving Stavroula frustrated by the forced delay in searching for the missing rooster until a more opportune moment. Spotting her newly found father Vasilis leading a watermelon laden Onos the donkey down the street, Stavroula called him over and told him to tether the donkey up and go on a hunt for her missing rooster.

"What it look like?" Vasilis asked.

"It look like a rooster of course" Stavroula told him "'ow many of 'em do you think are likely to be wandering around village."

"Well yous never know 'ows many there be" Vasilis insisted "give me proper description of bird."

Stavroula tried to recollect the physical appearance of the rooster, saying "It is orange with bright red comb on its 'ead and it makes a raucous din in the mornings. It 'as some black feathers on its rear end now I think of it."

"I looks then" Vasilis agreed, "but if Masha goes mad I is late 'ome with watermelons yous tell 'er it all yous fault."

"Whys you 'ave so many karpousi?" Stavroula asked, considering her newly found father appeared to have at least twenty massive fruits loaded onto the donkey which was visibly drooping under the weight.

"Masha read some rubbish watermelons are natural Viagra and insists on juicing 'em up and forcing me to drink it, seeds an' all. I'll be glad when they goes out of season as all that juice is playing 'avoc with my bladder" Vasilis lamented.

Chapter 16: A Smug Pappas And A Gorgeous Death

The Pappas was feeling very smug as his petition to prevent the local beach from turning into a haven for nudists had garnered many signatures. He considered he had acted with amazing aplomb by confronting two nude Scandinavian tourist women who had been frolicking shamelessly in the sea. As they emerged from the water without a stitch on he waded into the shallows to encase their naked bodies in a lobster adorned shower curtain grabbed from the windscreen of Tall Thomas' mobile refrigerated fish van, loudly chastising them with the words "Ladies, ladies, this isn't Lesvos you know."

Yiota from 'Mono Ellinka Trofima' had just arrived on the beach to take a refreshing dip and she applauded the Pappas' prompt action, while offering a toilet roll to wrap around the bits of the naked ladies the transparent shower curtain left exposed. The odious man went up in her estimation as she disapproved of nudity on public beaches and she applauded his vocal stance against it, promising to spread the word around. The Scandinavian tourists apologised for their error in mistaking the Astakos beach for a nudist one, assuring the Pappas they intended no offence as nudity was par for the course in their homeland.

Feeling satisfied with a good afternoon's work the Pappas rushed home to change into a clean clerical dress before heading to the church to siphon the rather scummy looking oil from the baptismal font into a bottle to proffer to the widow Mrs Christeas. He was relieved to discover Petula and the goat were not home and left them a quickly penned note saying he would be working late on churchly matters and not to wait up.

Passing the harbour-side kafenion he was surprised to be accosted by the local village men drinking coffee, as they usually ignored him. They voiced their concerns about the ghastly old crone Nitsa's arrest and wondered if he had any priestly advice on how they could help secure her release if Slick Socrates' lawyerly ministrations proved ineffective.

Although Nitsa was not particularly well liked in the village it was considered decidedly unjust and inhumane to imprison such a feeble yet spirited old lady. She was after all Tall Thomas' aunty. Moreover many of the villagers had argued vociferously with the man from the electric company over his flat out refusal to turn a blind eye to their efforts to fiddle their meter readings to reduce their bills.

Cleverly concealing his loathing of the frightful old woman the Pappas offered to start a petition demanding her release. He considered it fabulous news that Nitsa had been locked up in a prison cell and could not fathom why anyone would want to see her set free. Nevertheless if it would help improve his status in the village he was quite happy to abandon his very loose principles. Things were definitely going his way for a change.

Meanwhile Petula, the wife of the Pappas, was practising her driving techniques with Gorgeous Yiorgos but became overwrought when the pet goat Nero started to chew on her hair as she attempted a tricky hill start. As the car rolled suddenly backwards down the sharp incline she started to panic and Gorgeous Yiorgos suggested taking over the wheel to help her relax.

Gorgeous Yiorgos had been feeling out of sorts all day, suffering from a nasty case of indigestion and an aching arm. As the car crested the steep hill the sweat stood out on his brow and he suddenly slumped forward, losing control. Petula took one look at her companion and realised he had dropped dead from an instant heart attack. Remembering her first aid training she slammed all her weight into his back and the sudden sharp impact of the steering wheel on his chest jolted Gorgeous Yiorgos' heart back into action.

"What 'appened?" he wailed.

"Yous dropped dead and comes back to life, it is miracle" Petula told him. with tears rolling down her face.

"Does you cares then?" Gorgeous Yiorgos panted as his feeble heart made an effort to circulate blood through his system and he caught sight of her tears.

"I loves you Yiorgi" Petula declared, as the realisation she had almost lost this man who was so dear to her suddenly hit.

"I loves you too Petula my pet" Yiorgos cried, taking her in his arms in a loving embrace. "We must finds some way to free you from 'ideous marriage so wes can be together."

The romance of this miraculous moment was interrupted by Nero shoving his head between the couple and licking their faces with obvious approval at their budding romance.

Chapter 17: Crowded Out Of The Taverna

Mail order Masha strode into the kitchen wearing a silver sequin jumpsuit clinging sensually to her ample curves and demanded "Vasili sober up the donkey as we need to go out to eat, I 'ave 'ad no time today to cook the borscht."

Vasilis sighed in relief to be spared yet another dinner of Masha's burnt borscht and prised Onos the donkey's head out of a saucer of ouzo.

"You 'ave to wean donkey off ouzo" mail order Masha declared "pregnant donkey should not be boozing."

The mis-matched pair climbed onto the back of the tipsy donkey and made their way unsteadily into the village. Tethering the donkey outside 'Mono Ellinka Trofima' the pair were most put out to discover a mass of disgruntled locals on the taverna doorstep, complaining they could not get in to eat as every single seat was filled with Japanese tourists.

"Adonis he bring 'em along from 'is 'otel to eat 'ere and now there no room for us" Vangelis the chemist moaned.

"This is so dreadfully disappointing" said Quentin who had been looking forward to catching up with his village friends in what he now considered his local.

Peering through the open windows Prosperous Pedros passed on the information that every single Japanese tourist appeared to be eating a plate of green beans. "Appens they don't know this is Yiota's night for tripe soup. I 'ave been looking forward to 'er soup all day."

"Surely tripe soup isn't vegetarian" Deirdre opined.

"Of course it is Did-Rees, animals' insides bits don't count as meat" Prosperous Pedros insisted to Deirdre's amusement, as she struggled to visualize a plant growing a stomach.

"Perhaps if we wait they will finish up and leave" Tall Thomas suggested.

"I is not feeling patient" Prosperous Pedros stated. "I 'ad to go round my mother's 'ouse as she all in a flap over Nitsa's arrest. Your mother had cooked some foreign muck for dinner K-Went-In and tried to insist I eat it. That woman as mad as an hatter, no offence meant, but she 'ad concocted ice-cream out of potatoes and served it inside an oven cooked potato. Who in right mind eats potato ice cream?"

"Well actually Idaho potato ice cream is a highly acclaimed delicacy in our state" Deirdre said huffily.

"They says travel broadens the mind but dont's mentions it rots the stomach" Prosperous Pedros opined. "I wills sticks with 'ealthy Greek vegetarian diet what is 'ealthiest diet in world, even BBC says so, and avoid your mother's bizarre cooking."

"Did Fotini partake of mother's ice-cream?" Quentin questioned curiously.

"She ate 'ers and mine" Prosperous Pedros acknowledged in relief, recalling his mother's gluttony had spared him from tasting the obviously noxious frozen treat.

"So you have still never tasted any foreign food" Quentin pointed out, raising his eyebrows in amusement as Pedros replied, "No I is vegetarian."

Takis stepped outside the taverna to reassure the waiting crowd he hoped to empty the place of the Japanese tourists very soon. "They bin in 'ere two 'ours already but takin' long time to eat every green bean individually. Somebody runs and gets Bald Yannis as theys is eager to 'ave photographs with 'is goat an' it might encourage 'em to leave."

Takis had been delighted by the extra custom but did not want to risk losing his regulars to a rival taverna. He had suggested Adonis bring the Japanese much earlier another evening so they would be gone before the locals turned up.

Bald Yannis scowled at the news delivered by Tall Thomas that he was wanted at the taverna to round up a group of Japanese tourists and lure them to his shop. While he wanted their business he was still smarting over his ban from the taverna. He started to demand Tall Thomas tell Takis he would only oblige if Takis rescinded the ban, but Tall Thomas replied "suits yourself, is yous loss if they dont's take pictures with yous stupid goat."

"All rights, I come now" Bald Yannis finally agreed, mentally calculating how much money he could make from pimping his dressed up goat out for photographs.

The Japanese tourists departed the taverna clutching their selfie sticks, eager at the prospect of becoming social media stars pictured with the now famous goat Agapemini. The locals poured into the taverna and ravenously ordered platefuls of Yiota's aromatic tripe soup.

Gorgeous Yiorgos arrived and immediately claimed centre stage by dramatically recounting the details of his death earlier that day and his miraculous revival. The locals guffawed at his unlikely tale but he insisted he really had been dead and the honest Petula was his witness.

"Did yous see bright lights?" Vangelis the Chemist asked him.

"Wells it was pretty sunny" Gorgeous Yiorgos replied, refusing to be drawn into any religious nonsense.

"Wells people thoughts I was dead too but theys were wrong. At least they didn't try and bury you underground Yiorgo, that was most 'orrid moment of my life" that Old Fool Vasilis piped up, determined not to be outdone in the death defying experience department.

Taverna talk soon turned to the upcoming panagyri, a local festival celebrating naming the village after a lobster. All the fishermen planned on potting a huge lobster catch which would be cooked over an outdoor grill and shared by all the villagers. Quentin and Deirdre were visibly excited at the prospect of their very first Greek festival. Quentin volunteered to ask his mother to prepare Idaho potato ice cream to bring along but Prosperous Pedros put his foot down, insisting strange foreign foods would detract from the quintessential Greekness of the traditional occasion.

Slick Socrates commanded everyone's attention as he entered the taverna, slumping into a chair and calling out for a stiff ouzo. He reluctantly announced despite many tedious hours at the police station he had been unable to secure Nitsa's release. The poor old lady had been formally charged and transferred to the prison in the local town where she had undergone the indignity of a strip search before being thrown in a cockroach infested damp and mould ridden cell with a solitary light bulb, no running water and a lumpy mattress.

"At 'er advanced years I fears for 'er 'ealth in such 'orrid conditions, but officious policeman would not budge an' was determined to 'ave 'er locked up" Slick Socrates announced despairingly.

"Surely they will relent in the morning and let her go" Deirdre said.

"Did-Rees, there is precedent in Greece for chucking old people in prison cells" Socrates told her. "Not long back thirteen bulky policemen arrested unhealthy old man selling chestnuts without licence."

"Perhaps they will look more favourably on an old woman" Quentin suggested hopefully, concerned about his elderly neighbour's fate if she was left to rot in a prison cell.

His hopes were dashed when Socrates told him "being woman makes no difference. We alls remember whens eighty-years-old granny was arrested in Trikala for selling a few bunches of beetroots and broccoli without licence."

"She didn't go to prison though" Takis stated, recalling the famous case well.

"She got outrageous five thousand euro fine instead" Socrates mused.

"Was it a massive illegal vegetable empire she was illicitly running?" Quentin questioned, only to be told she had incurred the exorbitant fine for selling vegetables worth about thirty Euros she had dug up from her garden.

"Yous 'ave to remember old woman was dangerous tax evader depriving state of a few cents on sales" Prosperous Pedros added sarcastically. "Nows if theys really consider Nitsa drove illicit taxi illegally and dangerously, deliberately causing bodily 'arm to man from electric company, an' on top of that she didnt's declare taxes from exorbitant fares, theys mights well throw keys away. We 'ave to do something to get 'er out" he said stridently, thinking his mother may once again become unbearably demanding of him without Nitsa's companionship to distract her.

"The Pappas has arranged a village meeting for the morning to come up with a plan to release her if yous lawerly attempts were unsuccessful" Tall Thomas volunteered. "'Appen authorities will heed voice of clergy." He really hoped so as he had started to grow really fond of his old Aunty Nitsa who he considered an eccentric character.

"Well luckily no ones up in town will know of 'is terrible reputation so any 'elp he can give may carry some weight" Slick Socrates conceded as everyone agreed to meet first thing in the morning in the kafenion to hear the Pappas' plan.

"I bests be off early as I needs some sleep after deathly ordeal" Gorgeous Yiorgos announced as he took his leave, leaving the rest of the locals tucking despondently into tripe soup and mulling over the awful incarceration of the eighty two-year-old Nitsa. They fervently hoped she would survive the night in such horrendous conditions.

Chapter 18: Nitsa's Night In a Prison Cell

Nitsa was coping surprisingly well with her night in a prison cell though she had been mightily disappointed the handsome young prison guard with a thick moustache and a full head of hair had refused to strip search her, despite her protestations she was carrying illegal contraband in her bloomers. The other prisoners had voiced their disgust such a sweet old lady was being locked up and Nitsa was soon the recipient of all kinds of illegal prison goodies passed to her from the concerned inmates.

In no time at all she had the guards feeling sorry for her plight and had them running round fetching plates of moussaka and baklava. She demanded and received extra blankets and pillows, and insisted the guards disinfect her cell thoroughly before she could settle down for the night. She managed to wangle a private phone call to Fotini from the governor's office, during which she brazenly lied about her ordeal, describing her more than adequate lodgings as a flea ridden hell hole where she was being starved and brutally beaten.

Returning to what was by now the most comfortable cell in the prison she gratefully knocked back the contents of a bottle of brandy that had been smuggled inside. She proceeded to regale her fellow inmates with raucous stories before falling into a drunken stupor and then kept the rest of the prisoners awake all night with her stentorian snoring.

Chapter 19: The Pappas Goes Courting

"Like taking candy from a baby" Bald Yannis assured Moronic Mitsos as he described the pathetic eagerness of the Japanese tourists to be photographed with his pet goat Agapimeni and hand over their money for the pleasure.

"Mrs Kolokotronis did my darling proud with a lovely knitted ballerina skirt and matching bolero in lipstick pink" he confided. "She'll look a treat when theys put photos up online."

"Talking about online photos 'ave you found a new woman for me yet?" Moronic Mitsos asked, looking forward to any opportunity to cheat on his wife.

"As it 'appens I 'ave letter for yous from beautiful English school teacher what was very keen when I described you to 'er, mind yous I lied an' said yous was 'andsome" Bald Yannis told the moron.

Taking a leaf out of Hattie's 'catfisher' book he embellished his made up tale by telling Mitsos the woman was having problems exiting an African nation where she had been teaching English as a foreign language. She needed some cash funds transferring to her account in order to bribe her way out so the border guards would turn a blind eye to what had turned out to be a dodgy visa.

"Is she worth money?" Moronic Mitsos asked, to be assured by Bald Yannis that the English woman was indeed a stunner with an hourglass figure and a passion for retired Greek policemen with yachts.

Moronic Mitsos' interest was definitely piqued when Bald Yannis showed him a photograph he had printed from his computer of a totally random good looking woman. Mitsos considered the sum of two thousand Euros Bald Yannis told him was needed for the bribe would not make too big a dent in his generous police pension.

"Puts moneys in my bank account if you wants" Bald

Yannis suggested "and I send cash online to English woman as I knows you knows nothings about online banking."

"Is true I 'ave no ideas how these new fangled computer things work" Moronic Mitsos said. "If it no trouble to yous I puts cash in yous account in morning."

"Like taking candy from a baby" Bald Yannis said to himself, not quite believing how easy it had been to dupe the moron out of a couple of thousand Euros. He would transfer the cash to another of his accounts and then write a letter to Moronic Mitsos from the imaginary woman making another excuse for her inability to leave the African nation. He decided he must find out more details of how Hattie had been scammed so completely but realised an effective scam would probably necessitate him writing some gushing love letters to Mitsos.

As the two men chatted Gorgeous Yiorgos had left the taverna and started strolling home by the harbour. His interest was aroused by the sight of the Pappas furtively entering Thea's harbour- side house, clutching a bottle of olive oil. Recalling the house was now rented by a widow Yiorgos questioned what the Pappas could be up to at such a late hour and stealthily made his way to a side window where he had an excellent view into the kitchen of the harbour-side house. He decided if the Pappas was up to no good he could perhaps use it to his and Petula's advantage.

Mrs Christeas had the table ready laid and invited the Pappas to take a seat while she dished up the rooster in red sauce with noodles. The Pappas was dismayed when she accepted the proffered bottle of olive oil and insisting on opening it immediately poured a generous amount on top of the crusty bread he was about to consume. His mind immediately recalled the rather snotty brat he had dunked in the baptismal oil earlier in the week and he had no intention of letting any of the rancid fluid pass his lips.

"The rooster smells so good I believe I will forgo

the bread and oil" he declared, wincing in horror as Mrs Christeas took a hefty bite of her bread and pronounced the olive oil to be the elixir of the Gods. She waited with bated breath to see if the traditional courtship meal was acceptable to the Pappas' palate because if it did not pass muster he would be within his rights to leave the table and take his olive oil away with him.

Fortunately the Pappas tucked in with gusto. He could not fail to notice the admiration in the eyes of the handsome woman and he was most pleasantly surprised to find she did not move her leg away when he started to play footsie under the table.

"Where did you get this most excellent and tasty rooster?" he enquired, to which his hostess winked saucily and replied "ah, that would be telling." She had no intention of revealing the rooster was a stolen bird as she held the Pappas in high esteem and had no clue he had once turned his hand to burglary.

The Pappas could sense his luck was in as Mrs Christeas laughed heartily at his feeble rooster cock jokes and showered him with compliments, puffing up his own inflated sense of self importance. As he gnawed the last bit of rooster from the bone Mrs Christeas licked her lips suggestively and opened one of the buttons on her blouse. Before the Pappas had time to fathom her intent Mrs Christeas had thrown caution to the wind along with his clerical dress.

Poor Gorgeous Yiorgos was witness to the most hideous disrobing from his uncomfortable position hovering outside the window. He knew the horrendous sight of the 'in flagrante' couple would give him nightmares for weeks to come.

Chapter 20: The Upside Of Infidelity

Gorgeous Yiorgos lurked near the kafenion the next morning until he saw the Pappas arrive for the village meeting to discuss the plans to extricate Nitsa from prison. As soon as the coast was clear he headed to the Pappas' house to share the news he hoped would once and for all free Petula from her ghastly marriage.

"Petula my love I 'ate to be the one to tell yous but yous 'usband as been unfaithful to you."

"Would that were true but it can't be, who in her right mind would willingly have relations with my odious 'usband?" Petula laughed in disbelief.

"Is true my love, I sees it with my own eyes and believe me I wish I adn't as it was most orrible sight I ever seen."

"But who is the woman who would willingly go near 'im?" Petula questioned.

"It widow woman what is renting Thea's harbour-side 'ouse" Gorgeous Yiorgos revealed.

"That would be Mrs Christeas what is always 'anging round the church, I thought she was godly type, not an 'usband stealing floozy. But Yiorgi this is excellent news as perhaps now I can confront 'im and gets my divorce."

"Luckily I 'aves photographic evidence so he cannot deny 'is philandering" Yiorgos proudly declared, adding "my new fangled mobile phone 'as one of them new fangled cameras and I gots picture of 'em in revolting act."

"I can't bear to look" Petuala told him, adding "my 'usband is most revolting sight without his dress on."

Gorgeous Yiorgos had to agree as he took another look at the picture he had snapped of the Pappas stood in his knee-length grubby underpants and string vest, with his head squashed between Mrs Christeas' naked bosoms with what appeared to be a chicken bone and a feather sticking out of his ear.

"You must tells 'usband you know what he bin up to and demand divorce" Yiorgos said "an' if he gets difficult yous must threaten to takes photographic evidence of 'is adultery to slick lawyer."

"He 'ave to agree to divorce or I can threaten to make his carrying ons with widow public and he would get sacked from church for fornicating" Petula agreed. "I don't wants anything from 'im but my freedom and custody of goat."

"And when yous is free we can be married" Yiorgos declared "and in meantime yous can move in my 'ouse with me and we live in sin."

Petula's face was a picture of delight as she realised she had spent her last night trapped in her loveless marriage. Thanks to Gorgeous Yiorgos' clever snooping she had the grounds for the divorce she had dreamed of for so long and at last a chance of happiness with this kind hearted man she fallen in love with.

Chapter 21: Protest Plots

Stavroula woke up feeling out of sorts. She had overslept without the clamorous crowing of the rooster to serve as a natural alarm clock. Her plans to cook up Socrates' favourite meal and seduce him had been thwarted by that old fool Vasilis' inability to locate the missing rooster. Socrates hadn't even bothered coming home at a reasonable hour and when he did show up he had been preoccupied with his 'lawerly' failings to release Nitsa from prison and he failed miserably to perform his duties in the bedroom. Stavroula pondered the possibility of getting her hands on some of the Viagra mail order Masha force fed her husband.

Stavroula was now of the opinion her precious rooster had been stolen which meant she had to go to the bother of replacing it. She made a quick phone call to a man who kept birds in the village of Kokkoras, named for a rooster, and arranged for him to bring some choice birds over for her to make a selection from. Realising the cash outlay on new cocks would be wasted if there really was a rooster thief in the village prompted her to phone another man to negotiate the purchase of a vicious guard dog she could chain up outside the chicken coop.

She reflected if she'd had a guard dog it may have taken a bite out of the elusive underwear thief, but he appeared to have gone to ground. If he should ever reappear to continue his obsession with stealing bras and bloomers a guard dog would provide added protection for Stavroula's smalls. Unfortunately her plans were dashed as the dog man had not yet trained his latest beasts to be sufficiently vicious and so she would have to wait until their training was complete.

For once Socrates failed to look slick as he rushed off to the meeting at the kafenion. Stavroula's tardiness had left her no time to iron his bow tie and braces and he showed his displeasure by failing to kiss her as he left. Stavroula was incensed the meeting to discuss Nitsa's plight was being held in the kafenion rather than her own taverna, but it was organised by the Pappas who she had banned.

The Pappas was bursting with his own self-importance as he chaired the kafenion meeting. His mood was one of satisfied elation following the previous evenings encounter with the amorous widow. Slick Socrates made another call to the prosecutor's office and relayed the news the charges against Nitsa were so serious she would remain incarcerated until a trial could prove her innocence. As most of the judiciary were on one of their endless strikes Nitsa faced a very long spell behind bars, a desperate situation considering her advanced years. The Pappas' plan to start a petition to demand her release was approved by everyone, but the consensus was immediate and direct action was also needed to swing the arguments for her release in their favour.

The villagers were mulling over a variety of ideas when Toothless Tasos arrived back in the village. He had discharged himself from the hospital, cadging a lift from the smitten young doctor who was desperate to clap eyes once more on mail order Masha. Everyone stared in amazement at the bright green severed digit now sewn back onto Tasos' hand and made a mental note to demand a more competent surgeon if they ever needed sliced off body parts reattaching.

"Shoulds you be out of 'ospital so soon?" Petros the postman queried.

"I wants to be back 'ome with my Thea as miss 'er" Toothless Tasos explained. "Anyways I not like 'ospitals, they full of sickly types and bossy nurses what demands you take new fangled pills. I 'ave bottle of dangerous pills 'ere but refuses to take 'em as am strong as an 'orse" he said.

"Those dangerous pills are antibiotics which will stop your body developing a nasty life-threatening infection" Vangelis the chemist explained after studying the label.

"Taso you stupid" Bald Yannis interjected "everyone

knows you could drop dead of poisoned insides if yous refuses to takes antibiotics after surgery."

"I'd rather take my chances than swallow that muck" Toothless Tasos insisted, giving Bald Yannis a filthy look as it was his fan that had caused his medical emergency.

"Wells it be yous own funeral then" Vangelis the chemist stated.

"And thinks 'ow many men will tries to chat up Thea at your funeral. She wont's stay single long as never wastes time between dead 'usbands and is 'andsome woman" Fat Christos said.

As the truth of Fat Christos' convincing argument sunk in Toothless Tasos agreed to swallow the prescribed antibiotics as he could not bear the idea of Thea succumbing to the charms of a rival over his coffin. He struggled ineptly attempting to remove the child proof lid with his still useless finger until Fat Christos opened the bottle for him and Tasos reluctantly downed the pills.

The Pappas called "order" and said they had yet to resolve the issue of direct action over Nitsa. It was Quentin who came up with the ingenious idea of holding a protest outside the prison and suggested each villager devised a placard to wave.

"We could use slogan 'old crones' lives matter'" Bald Yannis suggested sarcastically, referring to the US 'black lives matter' movement which went completely over the other villagers' heads. He had no intention whatsoever of joining the protest as he was delighted Nitsa was safely behind bars and no longer able to cause havoc in his hardware shop. She had gone much too far on the last occasion she had bought goods from his shop by offering to pay in kind with her revolting old body.

His sarcasm went way over the villagers' heads and they agreed 'old crones' lives matter' was an excellent slogan to adopt for their protest.

"My sign will read 'free the Astakostan 1'" Quentin said, having recently watched a documentary about the Birmingham 6.

"I thinks it would be goodly idea to get giant photos of Aunty Nitsa and stick 'em on placards" Tall Thomas suggested to everyone's approval.

"'Ows we all gets to prison?" Toothless Tasos questioned as he didn't fancy paying a lot of money for transport to get there.

"We borrows bus from my cousin Adonis at the bus company" Adonis the mechanic declared to the universal approval of everyone. "I sees if he 'ave one free for this afternoon. Does I gets biglyy one? 'Ow many is coming on protest?"

Almost all of the villagers wanted in on the protest action as it would be the most excitement they had had for years and they relished the opportunity to voice their opposition to any form of authority. Bald Yannis and that old fool Vasilis refused to participate as they both loathed Nitsa, and Fat Christos put his foot down, insisting it was too dangerous for his pregnant wife Tassia and his mother to attend. Mrs Kolokotronis po poed him, asserting her right to show solidarity with another oldie by linking arms with Fotini and Hattie to demonstrate their mastery of holding firm against any attempts by the police to forcibly remove them from the protest.

Bald Yannis quickly spotted a commercial opportunity as he warned the villagers the police may well turn tear gas on them and he just happened to have a supply of rather musty old gas masks in the back of his hardware shop he could sell for a good profit. The meeting adjourned with everyone rushing into the hardware shop to buy protective masks for later in the day.

Chapter 22: Strange Greek Customs

Quentin and Deirdre decided to drive over to the 'Lemoni Spiti' to see how the renovations were progressing. They had several hours to kill before the bus was due to leave for the prison. Driving along the coastal road to Rapanaki their eyes drank in the stunning Greek scenery of turquoise sea water and ancient rock pools. Suddenly their attention was caught by a young woman who was washing her bedding in the sea.

"Oh Quentin, these must be desperate times indeed" Deirdre wailed. "Think how poverty stricken that poor young woman must be to have to resort to such measures. How much we take for granted whilst Greece is submerged in this dire financial crisis."

"How compassionate you are" Quentin said in admiration of his wife's empathy. "Let's stop and see if we can help in some way. At least we could give her some money so she can take her washing to the laundry rather than attempting to clean her bedding in such a primitive way."

Five minutes later they drove hurriedly away with the proverbial flea in their ears. They had interrupted the young woman in the post baptismal ritual of washing the sheet and towel which had been wrapped round her infant after his dunking in the very same church font full of Holy oil which Mrs Christeas had imbibed from the Pappas' home bottling. Tradition dictated these 'lathopana' were washed in the sea as the Holy oil is too precious to be washed out in a washing machine.

The young woman was mortified anyone could have the gall to presume she could not afford a washing machine and told the American pair in no uncertain terms they should get up to speed on traditional Greek customs before sticking their noses into other people's business.

Achilles the borrowed builder roared with laughter as

they explained their faux pas to him. He reassured them they'd had good intentions and the woman they had offered to help was a snobbish type who did not socialise in the village. "Anyone else would 'ave appreciated yous kind gesture was meants well and yous just ignorant of some of our traditional ways" he told them.

"Is work on the house progressing well?" Quentin asked him.

"Very goodly K-Went-In, comes and look at new chicken coop" Achilles said, leading the way towards a most luxuriant wooden structure in the garden.

"Well it's perfectly lovely but we rather hoped you'd go about making the house habitable before building somewhere for our non-existent chickens to live in luxury" Quentin said, reluctant to voice any criticism but peeved by the distraction.

"Well I builts it quick as 'eard on village gossip vine that bird man from Kokkoras is 'eading this way any day with some 'andsome roosters for sale. You won'ts get better cocks than 'is an' he dont's come this way verys often" Achilles explained.

Pointedly ignoring the subject of roosters Deirdre told him "we are off to town on the bus to participate in the prison protest. Will you be coming along Achilles?"

"Tries and keeps me away, I 'ate injustice and Nitsa isn't a bad old bird" Achilles replied. "In meantime I will get back to 'ammering new woods in place on bedroom ceiling to stops any vermin dropping on yous bed when yous in it and making Did-Rees shriek."

Back in Astakos Toothless Tasos arrived home to a warm welcome from Thea. He was delighted at the fuss she made over his finger and applauded the way she had not wasted any money on paying for transport to the hospital. He was less than delighted however when he discovered the kitchen bin was full of broken crockery. Thea admitted she loathed washing up dishes and instead smashed the dirty plates on the tile floor and then threw them away.

"This is profligate waste" Toothless Tasos admonished her "we nots living in a Greek wedding woman."

Thea defended her actions by telling Tasos she had a surfeit of crockery she had bought from the home shopping channel in the days when she was still a compulsive shopper. "We 'ave plenty of plates still left to break" she assured him, before he put his foot firmly down and told her there would be no more breakages and she could sell her excess plates to Stavroula for use in her taverna.

Over at the supermarket Fat Christos was doing a roaring trade in yoghurt as the villagers stocked up ready for their excursion to the prison. They intended to throw it at the prison guards to protest Nitsa's incarceration, having been inspired by the ancient Greek tradition of 'yiaourtoma', the noble art of chucking yoghurt at politicians.

The Pappas was writing a rousing speech about the inhumanity of imprisoning old women, which he hoped would win the approval of the church higher-ups, when Petula arrived at the church and dropped her bombshell.

"I knows you 'ave been 'aving adulterous relations with that church going widow Mrs Christeas and nows I want divorce" she told him.

The Pappas immediately denied his infidelity, claiming there was nothing going on between him and the widow. "'Ow easy lies trip off your tongue and yous supposed Godly man. Yiorgos 'ave photograph of you and widow doing unspeakable things on 'er kitchen table" Petula stated.

All the colour drained from the Pappas' face as he realised he had been caught in the act and photographic evidence could not be denied.

"This will ruin me if word gets out" he told Petula in a muted voice thick with apprehension.

"I don'ts want ruin yous, I'll only wants divorce and to

keeps goat" Petula said. "You can keeps your mucky secret and 'ouse too if yous give me divorce. I loves Yiorgos and we wills marry when I is free from yous."

"Yous promise not to blab in village about widow and me?" the Pappas begged her.

"I not blabs if yous go and sees Slick Socrates and make divorce official and gives me custody papers for Nero."

The Pappas realised he had no option other than to comply with Petula's demands. Since he had given up wine and wife beating his status in the village had begun to improve. He had his eye on the highest echelons of the church ladder and could not afford any new stain on his character becoming public knowledge. In truth he would be glad to rid himself of Petula though he felt sad at the prospect of losing Nero.

"Cans I at least 'ave access to goat on weekends?" he asked plaintively.

Chapter 23: The Prison Protest

"Po po Pedro, what is that most malodorously unpleasant pong?" mail order Masha demanded to know as Prosperous Pedros took his seat on the bus, laden down with the weight of a large bucket which stunk to high heaven.

"I brings rotted sardines to chuck at prison guards" Pedros revealed to the olfactory horror of all those who had the misfortune to be seated near him.

Mail order Masha had dressed for the occasion with great care as she considered Paraliakos, the town where the prison was located, to be the height of sophistication in comparison to the endless dullness of backwater Astakos. She could barely walk in her six inch heel stilettos and the skin tight red mini dress she had chosen was so tight it restricted her breathing, but did wonders for accentuating her silicone breasts and her impossibly long legs.

The smitten young doctor had managed to get an afternoon off from his hospital duties, pleading excruciating pain from his broken foot. He followed Masha onto the bus with his eyes glued greedily to her surgically enhanced bottom. She pouted at him in annoyance as she considered he ought to be more circumspect about his infatuation in public places as she was a married woman. She took a seat next to Evangelia from the beauty parlour and launched into conversation about the benefits of Botox, leaving the smitten young doctor stuck sitting next to Prosperous Pedros and his foul-smelling bucket.

The Pappas carried a large megaphone. Taking a seat on the bus far away from the widow Mrs Christeas he carefully avoiding eye contact with her, pointedly ignoring the seat she had saved for him. He wanted no hint of his involvement with her getting out for the villagers to gossip about. Petula had agreed not to make his philandering public knowledge if he agreed to a divorce. He realised he would need to be very discreet in any future assignations with the widow. The Pappas had a list of everyone who had signed up for the prison protest and stood up to call a register and tick off those present.

The villagers had done themselves proud with a high turnout in support of Nitsa. Local businesses were represented by Takis and Yiota from 'Mono Ellinka Trofima' and Stavroula from the rival taverna, Fat Christos and his mother Mrs Kolokotronis from the supermarket, Adonis the mechanic from the garage, Mr Mandelis from the jewellery shop and Vanglis the chemist from the pharmacy. The fishing contingent was boosted by the presence of Tall Thomas, Toothless Tasos and Gorgeous Yiorgos, while other earnest supporters of Nitsa's freedom included Achilles the borrowed builder, Petros the postman, Slick Socrates, Sotiris, Petula, Thea, Fotini, Hattie, Quentin and Deirdre.

Moronic Mitsos, in his capacity as the retired ex-chief of police, had pondered long and hard about joining the protest. He had been persuaded to come along by Bald Yannis who had decided at the very last minute to join the outing seeing as there would be no one left in the village to buy anything from his shop. He thought it might prove to be an amusing jaunt and he could always try to sabotage the protest.

As the Pappas finished taking the register he was surprised to see a number of Japanese tourists board the bus, mistaking it for a guided tour. Thinking they would help to boost the protest numbers he let them stay and instructed the bus driver to set off towards town. The bus had barely started to roll when Adonis flagged it down and jumped aboard, determined to stick close to his Japanese guests and attempt to sell them a house, even though they could barely understand a word he said.

The villagers had made so many placards reading "Free the Astakostan 1", "Old Crones' Lives Matter" and "We / Nitsa" they had plenty to spare for the rather baffled Japanese tourists who thought it most generous the villagers were gifting them these incomprehensible signs. They signified their gratitude by beaming politely and offering the other bus passengers strips of dried seaweed they had pocketed as delicious snacks and which drew many curious glances. Fotini mistook the green square of seaweed as a pocket handkerchief and blew her nose noisily into it, while Hattie used her piece to mop her sweaty brow as she had still not acclimatised to the scorching Greek temperatures.

As the bus began to wind its way up the hairpin mountain bends Mrs Christeas stuck her head out of the window and vomited violently. She reasoned she couldn't be sick from the previous evening's meal of red rooster as the Pappas had eaten the same dish and appeared in rude health. She had no idea his offering of olive oil had been tainted with the ghastly germs of the snotty brat who had been dunked in the supposedly Holy oil the cheapskate Pappas had bottled. The smitten young doctor was summoned to the widow's side to aid her but she promptly threw up all over his trousers.

The combined smell of musty rubber from the gas masks, rotten sardines and vomit, all made for a very unpleasantly malodorous journey and the villagers fought each other to be the first to get off the bus when it pulled up in Paraliakos square opposite the prison. The Japanese tourists were far too polite to elbow their way out of the bus and were the last to descend into the confused commotion, but were soon rounded up to join the circular march constituting the protest.

The protestors' rowdy cries of "Free Nitsa" soon attracted the attention of the prisoners who were on their exercise period in the prison yard. The prisoners lost no time in hoisting Nitsa onto their shoulders from where she screeched words of encouragement to her fellow villagers. The guards, woken from their afternoon nap, were taken by surprise and unsure whether to point their rifles at the prisoners or the protestors.

The raucous noise soon stirred the locals and before very long an enterprising kiosk owner hoping for a backhander summoned the local television station to come along to film the protest. As the camera crew filmed the now preening protestors shaking their placards in the air the reporter was busy trying to find the best representative from the protestors to interview for this breaking news story. Although the Pappas was in charge of the protest he was dismissed as far too unphotogenic to speak on camera. The reporter honed in on mail order Masha's plastic beauty and she was delighted to be thrust into the spotlight.

"We is protesting the unjust arrest and incarceration of Astakostan Nitsa, an innocent old woman what 'as been treated disgustedly by authorities" Masha said. "All she dids was accidentally knock electric man off pole and for that she 'as been strip-searched and tortured. She is over eighty an' should be at 'ome with other old crones she lives with. It not as if electric man is even dead."

Fotini elbowed Masha roughly out of the way and piped up "electric man deserve what he got, he cut off me electric supply. Nitsa and me 'ave no lights in 'ouse and were victims of murdering rapist what tried to burns 'ouse we live in down. Police does nothing 'bouts it then arrests poor Nitsa whats is innocent. Wheres justice in that?"

The reporter was in his element at this wonderful scoop of such an obvious miscarriage of justice. He decided to play up the victimisation of innocent old women as his angle, compounded by the incompetence of the police in failing to arrest the nasty criminal who had obviously terrorised them.

Hattie pushed her way forward and linked arms with Fotini, declaring on camera in excruciatingly mangled Greek she intended to bring this miscarriage of justice to the attention of the American Embassy. The reporter got overly excited when he realised the protestors included Americans and upon spotting the Japanese, who had no idea at all what they were actually protesting but were quite happy to wave their placards, he realised he had the makings of an international story that could make him famous across the world. He decided to exploit the story for all it was worth, never questioning Nitsa's actual guilt or the ridiculous claims she had been strip- searched, starved and beaten.

On the other side of the prison wall the prisoners refused to return to their cells and joined in the calls to free Nitsa. The prison governor was watching the protestors spread their lies on the television in his office and rushed outside flanked by two burly prison guards to put his side of the story to the reporter. Pushing his way in front of the camera the prison governor insisted Nitsa was receiving the best treatment possible. The reporter interjected to question "but do you deny an innocent eighty-two year old woman who has not many years left on this earth is locked up in your prison and has been starved and tortured?"

"Well she is old is true and is technically locked up, but is 'aving the best of treatment" the governor replied "and it is not proven she is innocent of charges."

"Innocent until proven guilty" the protestors began to chant while taking the opportunity to lob smelly sardines and yoghurt at the governor and his guards.

The governor and his flunkies hastily fled back into the safety of the prison compound, doused in yogurt and rotten stinking sardines, totally humiliated by their very public 'yiaourting'. The governor immediately telephoned the chief of the Paraliakos police to demand a riot squad be deployed to disperse the protestors with tear gas. The police chief had been glued to the television coverage and had been guffawing uncontrollably at the sight of the prison governor and guards being 'yiaourted'. He argued tear gassing the protestors may be overkill as the protestors were not ripping up paving slabs or breaking shop windows. However the governor's pride had been dented and he insisted his demands were acceded to immediately, reminding the police chief he had the ear of the mayor.

As the reluctant riot squad arrived and prepared to fire tear gas at the protestors the Astakostans and the Americans pulled on the gas masks they had precautionarily purchased from Bald Yannis. The unprepared Japanese tourists were the only ones to suffer from the tear gas attack, apart from Bald Yannis who had neglected to buy one of his own protective devices and the Pappas who was determined to act like a martyr to the cause.

The tear gassing of the Japanese tourists soon prompted a major international incident as they were filmed prostrate on the ground hacking painfully while temporarily blinded. This instantly put Astakos on the map and won Nitsa legions of worldwide fans who thought she looked like a sweet old granny in the blown up photographs the protestors waved. The international audience immediately wrote to their governments demanding they intervene diplomatically to free the charming old dear.

Chapter 24: Nitsa Revels In Her Torture

The villagers decided it would be prudent to spend another hour in Paraliakos before heading back on the bus to Astakos, enabling the Japanese tourists' time to seek medical attention from the smitten young doctor for the noxious effects of the tear gas. Bald Yannis, being made of sterner stuff, pushed the smitten young doctor aside and being on safer ground headed off to the nearest washing line as he was feeling nostalgic and fancied a spot of underwear stealing.

Tall Thomas took the opportunity to bribe a prison guard with a freshly caught swordfish providing he would ensure Aunty Nitsa received a bottle of brandy to help her sleep and a lobster adorned patriotic shower curtain to use as a bedspread to make her feel more at home. Mail order Masha used her ample charms on another guard who willingly agreed to sneak some cosmetics in to Nitsa. Masha could imagine nothing worse than being locked up without anything to slap on her face. As she touched up her own lipstick the by now smitten young reporter persuaded her to let him whisk her off for an intimate dinner in an expensive taverna and she told the others to tell Vasilis she would be home later. The smitten young doctor boarded the bus in a foul temper as the object of his affections was proving so fickle.

The Pappas wished the widow Mrs Christeas would stop winking so obviously at him. As soon as the bus took off she resumed vomiting out of the window, leaving him temporarily safe from her advances. The villagers were satisfied their protest was all over the television news and hoped international public opinion would soon sway the authorities to release Nitsa.

Meanwhile Nitsa was basking in all the attention. The prison governor was so worried all the adverse publicity may reflect badly on him he set up a bed in his office for Nitsa before heading home to shower off the yoghurt, completely forgetting this would give her total access to his telephone. In no time at all she was ordering take away food to be delivered to the prison gates and conducting interviews over the phone with every television station she could contact.

She was in her element as she described how the prison guards had put her on a rack. She revelled in her ludicrous account of being stretched from limb to limb, before being hung from a hook in the prison dungeon and whipped mercilessly. The horrified prison governor listened as Nitsa wrapped the easily duped saps at Amnesty International round her little finger. It came as no great surprise when the Minister of Prisons telephoned him in a great fury and announced he was sacked for gross incompetence.

Chapter 25: In Pursuit Of A Generous Dowry

On his return to Astakos Bald Yannis settled in behind the hardware shop counter. Hoping he wouldn't be disturbed by any annoying customers he started to pen a love letter to Moronic Mitsos. Chewing on the end of his ballpoint and rubbing his still painful tear gassed eyes he tried to come up with something romantic to write, but admitted to himself such nonsense really was not his forte. Having been single all his life Bald Yannis was clueless how to approach women so his literary efforts were rather dire, though to his credit he was soon able to emulate the best of the 'catfishers' as their missives tended to be appalling.

"I am absolutely impressing to see your handsome looks" his letter began "and I find it difficult to get you out of my mind."

He hoped he sounded like a besotted female English school teacher. It was important he was convincing if he was to successfully extract more money from the moron. His missive continued "You look so nice, so manly, with a smiling outlook and every woman knows something good must appreciate the good creature in you. If you were a flower I would not pick you but grow you in the garden and cultivate and smell you."

His soppy masterpiece was interrupted by the arrival of Toothless Tasos seeking compensation for losing his finger in the lethal blades of the fan. "You can't claims money" Bald Yannis sneered, pointing at the newly penned shop sign declaring "If yous loses fingers in fans, hardware shop not liable for yous stupidity."

"I wills ave to see what Slick Socrates says abouts that" Toothless Tasos said huffily, adding "least yous can do is gives me free turpentine to get green pain off finger."

"If turpentine worked does you thinks I'd still be walking round with this 'ere green hand?" Bald Yannis retorted, waving his green hand in the air. "It wills take years for green resilient boat paint to come off. I coulds sells yous some sandpaper to rubs top layer of skin off I supposes."

Toothless Tasos handed over the cash for a large sheet of sandpaper and went on his way, muttering he would see Bald Yannis in court. It was all hot air though as he had no intention of handing over any of his hard earned money to that charlatan lawyer Socrates.

"Po po, I 'ave lost my romantic thread" Bald Yannis muttered under his breath, while stroking his pet goat Agapemini for inspiration. The feel of the goat's warm flesh plus the strain of composing a love letter made him wonder if he was missing out by remaining single. If he got himself a wife he could put her to use around the house and in the shop. The more he thought about it the more the idea of acquiring a wife suddenly appealed to him, especially the idea of a wife with a substantial dowry. She would need to be able to cook tasty vegetarian food, be good with a scrubbing brush and never nag him or answer him back.

He began to wonder how one actually went about finding a wife as he wasn't gullible enough to fall for a scammer on the internet like Moronic Mitsos and Hattie had done. He supposed he would have to actually meet a woman and woo her, but he had no idea how to go about it. The only woman to show any interest in him in the last decade was the frightful old hag Nitsa and he wasn't that desperate.

Suddenly it occurred to him that the old fashioned custom of using a matchmaker would most likely suit his purpose. He decided to strike while the iron was hot and telephoned an old aunt of his in a high-up mountain village who had had much success in pairing up the most difficult to match people. He told her "I is after a wife what is not shy of hards work and who 'as generous dowry. I dont's cares 'ow ugly she looks as long as she's not mouthy nagging type."

His aunt promised to draw up a list of wifely candidates

for Bald Yannis to vet. With the matter resolved he went back to his letter and began to describe his voluptuous womanly figure and his shiny long hair to Moronic Mitsos.

Chapter 26: The Parrot Parrots Some Home Truths

Stavroula was screaming at Slick Socrates in the taverna kitchen. The sea salt she had asked him to collect from the rock pools by the sea had a nasty yellow tinge which her customers would be rightly suspicious of.

"'Ow was I to knows goats had peed in rock pool water?" Socrates said in his defence "'appen customers won't notice and if theys do just tells 'em it is exotic salt."

Their argument was interrupted by the arrival of old Kyrios Kokkoratis from the village of Kokkoras, who pulled up outside the taverna in a pick-up truck piled high with cages of hens and roosters. Stavroula was delighted to have the first pick of the crop of cocks and plumped for a dozen very plump specimens. She chose some fine egg laying hens to complement the roosters and settled the new birds comfortably in the chicken coop. She smiled to herself as the coop reminded her of the final resting place of her second husband Kostas, which the bungling policemen from Pouthena had been too incompetent to discover.

"Where does I find the Americans what wants some birds?" Kyrios Kokkoratis asked. As luck would have it Quentin and Deirdre were having coffee in Stavroulas with Hattie and Fotini. In no time at all Quentin was persuaded to buy several hens and roosters to house in the new chicken coop Achilles the borrowed builder had built in the garden. Although both he and Deirdre were totally clueless in the art of chicken keeping Fotini assured them she would look after the birds in exchange for freshly laid eggs.

Kyrios Kokkoratis was busy trying to squash all the now cage free birds into Quentin's car. It was quite a squeeze with Quentin and Deirdre in the front, and Hattie and Fotini on the back seat with hens and roosters on their knees and pecking around their feet. Fotini screeched "keep your 'ands to yourself yous pervert" as Kyrios Kokkoratis brushed up against her, attempting to squeeze the last bird into the livestock packed car.

"Keep your 'ands to yourself yous pervert" resounded in the air as something perfectly mimicked Fotini's words in a high pitched squawking tone.

"That the parrot talking, it quick study" Kyrios Kokkoratis explained, asking the foursome " does yous wants sees it?"

Quentin and Deirdre had no interest in viewing the parrot. They wanted to get home as quickly as they could to escape the close proximity of their chicken cargo and its very distinctive fowl smell. Fotini had other ideas though and insisted on viewing the parrot, to which she took an instant liking. Testing its verbal skills she said "Quentin is gormless" and to her great delight the parrot responded "Quentin is gormless, Quentin keep your 'ands to yourself you pervert, Quentin is gormless."

Fotini cackled happily. She was quite entranced by the parrot and most determined to have it. Catching sight of her son Prosperous Pedros drinking coffee in the kafenion she insisted Quentin toot his horn to attract his attention. "What is it now mother?" Pedros queried hoping his mother wasn't about to make any unreasonable and time consuming demands.

"Cans yous pay for this 'ere parrot Pedro and I pays yous back when I gets my meagre pension?" Fotini asked.

Prosperous Pedros launched into keen negotiations over the price of the parrot with Kyrios Kokkoratis who was actually desperate to be to be rid of the foul mouthed creature. Satisfied he had got the parrot for a bargain price Pedros told his mother the bird was his gift to her and she need not part with any of her meagre pension. "Yous is good son Pedro" Fotini said warmly "comes by 'ouse and I cooks yous up fresh eggs what these 'ere hens will lay."

As Quentin drove past the hardware shop Fotini taught

the parrot to say "Bald Yannis fancies Nitsa" and by the time they drove past the church the parrot was word perfect as it shrilled "the Pappas is a drunken wife beater."

The parrot could not have picked a more inopportune moment to accuse the Pappas of being a drunken wife beater as he was at that very minute welcoming some higher-ups from the church in his most grovelling manner. The professional image he was striving to project with his eye on a promotion up the church ladder was shattered as he shouted "shut up yous malaka" at the parrot. Clapping a hand over his mouth he apologised profusely to the bishop for his use of the common expletive.

Ignoring the parrot's accusations completely the Pappas launched into a self-promoting monologue, extolling his great success in petitioning against the nudist beach to keep the children safe from such wanton lewdness. He explained to the bishop how he been elected in the role of village leader to petition for the release of an innocent old lady who had been thrown into prison, as it was the Godly and humane thing to do. The bishop was beginning to look suitably impressed when Slick Socrates suddenly burst into the church, proclaiming "About times you agreed to divorce Petula, she well rid of yous. I needs yous to sign these 'ere papers to get divorce rolling."

Without saying a single word the Pappas put his signature on the papers while pushing Socrates hastily out of the door. Turning back he was horrified to note the look of complete disapproval on the bishop's face and blurted out "I 'ave to divorce wife on accounts she is fornicating with another man."

The bishop immediately sympathised with the cuckolded Pappas, telling him "divorce is the business of the anti-Christ but it is a terrible sin when a married woman fornicates with another man. Perhaps if I had a serious talk with her and can persuade her to fall at your feet and beg your forgiveness you could consider taking her back."

The Pappas blanched at the prospect of the bishop finding out from Petula that she was in fact the innocent party and it was he that had been caught out on camera fornicating on the kitchen table with the amorous widow. If the bishop found out he was the actual sinner his days in the church would be over. Not only would he be out of his job but out of the house that came with his churchly position.

"Please no, do not think of troubling yourself Bishop, my wife 'as gone too far on path of sin to deserve redemption. Is best we parts ways and I dedicate my future life to God with no wifely distractions" the Pappas pleaded. "Luckily we 'aves no children to consider."

"Well if you are sure the marriage is over you may have your divorce from the adulterous floozy" the bishop said "but you know you will have to remain single as cannot remarry in the eye of the church."

"I have no interest in women, only God" the Pappas lied through his teeth, hoping the bishop would not stay much longer as he was already late for his secret rendezvous with the amorous widow Mrs Christeas.

Chapter 27: Filthy Foreign Food Muck

That old fool Vasilis was fit to burst with pride when he saw his beautiful young bride being interviewed live on the television news. However his mood soon turned sour when he spotted the smitten young doctor ministering to the tear gassed Japanese tourists as he jealously didn't want him anywhere near his wife. Climbing onto Onos the donkey he headed into the village, hoping to find mail order Masha drinking vodka in 'Mono Ellinka Trofima'.

"She stopped up in town to 'ave dinner with that young reporter" Yiota told him "an' if yous wants food we only 'aves lamb chops tonight as I 'ad no time to cooks when protesting."

Vasilis frowned in annoyance, suspecting his wife was actually embroiled in a secret assignation with the smitten young doctor. Remembering her temper tantrum when he had falsely accused her of carrying on with the doctor, he decided to give her the benefit of the doubt as the least expensive option. He was inordinately pleased when the other villagers told him Masha looked like a movie star on the television. He decided he would give her the money to pay for the cheek fillers she had been hinting at for weeks.

The other villagers were all tucking into Takis' aromatic grilled lamb chops. Curious eyes settled on Deirdre when she surreptitiously pulled a jar of shop bought green sludge from the depths of her handbag and spooned it liberally over her meat.

"What's that you puttings on lamb Did-Rees?" Tall Thomas asked her, to which Deirdre replied,

"It is mint sauce, a most delicious condiment to pair with lamb."

. "Sounds like one of them peculiar foreign ways of messing with good Greek foods that cannot be improved with anythings but oregano" said Prosperous Pedros, gnawing heartily on a vegetarian lamb chop liberally doused with a squeeze of fresh lemon. As the jar was passed round from table to table everyone agreed the notion of mint sauce was most peculiar. The locals sniffed it suspiciously before denouncing it as filthy foreign food muck which had no place on a good Greek table.

"You'lls learn Did-Rees" Takis told her. "Yous need to adapt to Greek ways now yous living 'ere. Yous dont's wants be mistaken for them tourists what asks for grilled children when they means to order lamb chops" he chortled, recounting how many foreign people confused 'paidakia' with 'paidia' through simple mispronunciation.

"Next you'll expect me to wash my bedding in the sea" Deirdre said, but her joke went completely over their heads and they asked if she was planning on having Quentin baptised.

"I have no intention of letting the odious Pappas dunk me in his oily font" Quentin quipped.

As soon as the Pappas was mentioned the villagers began to gossip about his impending divorce from Petula. They unanimously agreed the lovely Petula was well rid of the Pappas and speculated if she and Gorgeous Yiorgos were now a romantic item.

Fat Christos stared wistfully at the lamb chops as his diet was still restricted to liquidised foods. It had been months since he had tasted anything solid and he was beginning to hanker after his mother's unhealthy liquidised delights. The only thing preventing a dietary lapse was the memory of the agony he endured when his stapled stomach had a close encounter with liquidised sausages and spinach pies. He sipped his water and enjoyed the company of his friends. He hoped their chatter would take his mind off his mother's poisonous references to the true paternity of Tassia's unborn child and her snide remarks about which of the villagers the baby would resemble. He was content in his new marriage and his ownership of a burgeoning supermarket empire, but his mother's constant hints he was not the father of Tassia's baby was grating on his nerves.

He could live with the fact Tassia had most likely already been pregnant before he had the rather sweaty encounter with her in the garden shed, but he was concerned his mother's suspicions would get out and upset Tassia. His marriage to her had brought him enough money to give up his life of fishing and become a man of, admittedly thin, substance. He had grown fond of Tassia and her unassuming ways and he did not want her to be shamed. He wondered if there was any way to find out who the father was so he could buy his silence and preserve Tassia's secret for eternity, but he had no clue who she had done the guilty deed with.

Adonis slunk into the taverna shrouded in a mood of abject self pity. The Japanese tourists had barricaded themselves into their hotel rooms and refused to come out as they were fearful for their lives after the violent encounter with the riot police. Adonis was worried future tourists from Japan would cancel their bookings due to the negative publicity of the tear gassing incident.

"I bets if yous persuaded Bald Yannis to take 'is precious goat to visit 'em in 'otel they woulds come rounds" Takis suggested to Adonis' great delight, surmising the solution was perfect. Adonis phoned Bald Yannis and offered him an enormous bribe to get out of his bed and take the pet goat down to the hotel. As both men had a vested interest in fermenting an abiding interest in Astakos from the Japanese they were able to come to a cordial arrangement. In no time at all Agapimeni was being paraded between hotel rooms in her knitted finery. Her celebrity presence calmed the tourists so much they agreed to write nice things about the village on their social media accounts and play down the awfulness of being gassed.

"Ere turns up the telly" Tall Thomas demanded as the

news coverage was showing highlights of the prison protest.

"There's my Masha" that old fool Vasilis said with pride, but he was shushed as everyone wanted to listen closely to the telephone interview Nitsa was giving from the prison governor's office.

"Oh dear we must do more to get old aunty out" Tall Thomas wailed "she's in no fit 'ealth to survive the rack and starvation."

"The canny old crone is pulling their legs" Yiota asserted "if they's really torturing 'er I'll eat Did-Rees revolting mint sauce. Listen to 'ow that useful idiot from Amnesty International is 'anging on 'er every word, what a plonker. She just saying all this rubbish to get sympathy vote and lets us keep fingers crossed it works. Slick Socrates is checking back with authorities in morning so we'lls know more then."

"I best be off in case Masha goes straight 'ome to 'ouse" that old fool Vasilis announced. Seeing mail order Masha on television had stirred something in him that had not been naturally roused since his honeymoon. Climbing onto Onos the donkey he tossed his bottle of Viagra into the sea.

Chapter 28: The Housekeeper

Without a wife to return home to the Pappas cast caution to the wind and spent the night with the amorous widow Mrs Christeas in her rented harbour-side house. He had moved up in the world from fumbling around on her kitchen table to a place in her bed. He was rudely awoken the next morning, even before Stavroula's new roosters could start crowing, by someone banging loudly on the front door. Crawling across the bedroom floor on his elbows to avoid detection he cast a furtive glance out of the window and spied two burly men beating forcefully on the door demanding entrance.

The widow Christeas was horrified at the prospect of anyone catching her in her hair curlers and demanded the Pappas get rid of the unwanted visitors. The Pappas turned on her, angrily crying "are you demented woman, it's more than my jobs worth if anyone finds out I spent the night in yous bed. Yous get rids of them while I climbs out of kitchen window."

Mrs Christeas was most put out by the Pappas acting in such an unchivalrous manner and almost ignored his request to throw his dress out of the window after him. Throwing a towelling robe over her formidable form she thrust open the front door and demanded to know what the burly men wanted at such an unspeakable hour. "We are debt collectors come to take furnishings as yous have failed to honour yous monthly commitments to home shopping channel" they told her.

"I 'aves never bought anything from that ungodly channel" Mrs Christeas proclaimed "and as a good Christian woman I nevers use credit."

"Wells that's as maybe but we 'ave official paper to repossess all furniture in this 'ere 'ouse" insisted the debt collectors, flaunting the paperwork in the widow's face.

"It is Thea not me what owes this money" the widow told

them after inspecting their papers. "She owns this 'ouse and I pays 'er good rent money to lives 'ere."

"Well fact is its 'er furniture and we're taking it" the debt collectors said as they began to carry the kitchen table out of the house. The loud commotion they were making raised the other villagers from their beds and Mrs Christeas was mortified to realise there was now a large audience to witness this unspeakable humiliation.

Forgetting all about her hair curlers she strode through the village in her dressing gown to beat at Toothless Tasos' door. Tasos was just about to go fishing and was not pleased to be disturbed by this strident woman shrieking Thea had conned her. "'Ows I supposed to live without furniture?" the widow demanded to know.

Tasos had no idea what she was talking about as Thea's house was fully furnished. "Not anymore it not as debt collectors 'ave carted it all off" Mrs Christeas insisted.

"There must be some mistake" Toothless Tasos attempted to assure her as he knew the money Thea earned from her knitting was used to pay off the money owed to the home shopping channel in monthly instalments. Attempting to push the widow away from his house Toothless Tasos offered her the loan of his deck chair, but she was having none of it and demanded to see Thea immediately. Thea, however, had snuck out of the back door when she heard the commotion, not wanting to face Toothless Tasos and admit to him her debts had once again got the better of her as she had been on a spontaneous spending spree.

The Pappas was none too pleased to see Mrs Christeas enter the sanctuary of the church still clad in her dressing gown and rollers. "'Ows I supposed to live in 'ouse with no furniture" she screeched "and with no bed for us to romp in?"

The Pappas was desperate to shush her in case she was overheard but cannily came up with the ideal solution. Now

Petula had left him to live with Gorgeous Yiorgos he was finding the housework was piling up and he had no intention of doing it as he considered it quite beneath him. He could not openly acknowledge his relationship with the amorous widow but was sure the bishop would understand were he to engage the services of a live-in housekeeper.

"Yous can move in with me as 'ousekeeper" he invited. "I can'ts pays yous but yous will save money on rent." He also considered it far less dangerous than sneaking in and out of the harbour-side house where he had already been caught 'in flagrante' by Gorgeous Yiorgos' camera.

Mrs Christeas immediately saw the sense in the Pappas' suggestion. If she lived under his roof it would be far easier for her to get her claws permanently into him and she imagined it would improve her standing in the village if she was to become the housekeeper to what she wrongly presumed was a respected man. The savings she would make on the rent money would leave more disposable income from her meagre pension and the Pappas' house had a garden where she could hide any pilfered hens and roosters.

Pleased with the prospect of her new living arrangements Mrs Christeas told the Pappas he could expect his favourite meal of village rooster in red sauce with macaroni waiting for him at home that evening. Striding briskly back to the harbour-side house to pack up her clothes she took a shortcut through Stavroula's garden where she helped herself to one of the new roosters and secreted it under her dressing gown.

Chapter 29: Bald Yannis Talks Women

The following day Bald Yannis was busy straightening bent out of shape second hand nails with a hammer to sell as new stock when he received a call from his aunt the matchmaker. She wanted him to meet an impoverished farmer who still had four unmarried daughters to get off his hands. The family lived in a high and remote mountain village abandoned by most people under pensionable age as it offered no work opportunities for young people.

The only remaining inhabitants under the age of seventy were these four spinster sisters who still lived at home, where their father kept them busy tending the farm he ruled with a rod of iron. With a dwindling income the father had now decided he needed to lose a daughter or three to marriage to reduce his outgoings, keeping at least one of the four unmarried to tend to him in his dotage. He was prepared to offer a dowry of one hundred goats and some olive trees that had ceased being profitable.

The phone call threw Bald Yannis into a panic. Pondering if he could really go through with his plans to acquire a wife he muttered "I'd best seek advice from men in kafenion what have more experience with women as they is alien creatures to me."

"Aving Thea in my life 'as been blessing and curse" Toothless Tasos confided. "She make 'ouse a 'ome and I loves her, but she 'as no sense when it comes to spending. She bigly improvement on first wife Stavroula who nag me to death an' Thea dont's makes any demands in bedroom." Recalling Stavroula's voracious sexual appetite he compared it in his mind to Thea's adamant refusal to let him canoodle until their situation was legal.

"Petula is a ray of sunshine in my life and I loves 'er dearly" Gorgeous Yiorgos boasted "but it tooks me three wives before I finds right woman. 'Appen you takes risk

Yanni if you marry first woman what comes along."

"I thinks yous is mad to even thinks of giving up goodly single life" Prosperous Pedros butted in. "I for ones will never marry."

"But yous is prosperous enoughs to not see attraction of dowry" Toothless Tasos said, wishing Thea had come with a dowry rather than a pile of debts.

"Wells I thinks matchmaker is goodly idea" Tall Thomas interjected "I quite likes thought of 'aving a wife but 'ave no idea where to finds one. An 'andsome woman to keeps bed warm and cooks up goodly meals 'as quite an appeal to me an' I is sicks of being alone."

"I not bother if she 'andsome or nots as long as dowry is" Bald Yannis told him. "Looks is over rated."

"Lets 'ope woman thinks same as no ones will ever falls for yous with your ugly bald 'ead and lack of all charms" Gorgeous Yiorgos said smugly, recalling how many women he had captivated with his Greek godlike looks when younger.

"Yous says matchmaker found man with four daughters" Tall Thomas said "perhaps I coulds 'ave second pick whens you sorted out business with 'im Yanni."

Bald Yannis calculated he could save some cash on the matchmaker's commission if he took Tall Thomas along and she found him a wife too. It would also make the dreaded encounter with the four unwed daughters less daunting if he had Tall Thomas along for Dutch courage. "Yous can comes too if yous like but I 'aves first pick of crop" he agreed.

"Yous 'ardly likely to win hearts if yous call 'em crops" Gorgeous Yiorgos said in disgust. "At least shows some respect when you meets 'em. Most likely they will 'ave feelings and wants be told they are fragrant flowers, not treated like goats."

"I treats my goat like princess" Bald Yannis declared.

"Wells tries and do same when you meet prospective

wife" Gorgeous Yiorgos advised. Annoyed at the reprimand Bald Yannis took the words to heart and decided if he found any of the four sisters suitable he would make her a lovely and thoughtful gift of some stolen underwear.

Chapter 30: Watermelon and Botox Weapons

That old fool Vasilis had stayed up half the night waiting for mail order Masha to return from her dinner with the young reporter in Paraliakos. Peering from the window hoping to spot his beloved return he caught sight of a figure lurking suspiciously beneath an orange tree and wondered if it could be the elusive underwear thief, who still remained at large, hoping to make a grab for Masha's lace knickers. Grabbing a watermelon from the kitchen as a possible weapon he stepped outside to confront the lurker.

The smitten young doctor, having nodded off while waiting to catch a glimpse of the object of his desire, was caught unaware by Vasilis. He was woken abruptly when Vasilis dropped the heavy watermelon onto his broken foot and demanded to know "what's yous doing 'anging round 'ere at this late 'our?"

"Now hold on, there's no need for violence old man" the smitten young doctor cried, clutching his foot in agony. "I was simply waiting for Masha as she mentioned she would like Botox injections."

"An' no doubt you planned to stick 'er with yous needle in dead of night" Vasilis retorted, demanding "shows me evidence now."

The smitten young doctor had taken the precaution of arming himself with a Botox filled syringe just in case of such an eventuality. Vasilis grabbed the syringe and jabbed it violently in the skin directly beneath his rival's mouth. "That will put paid to yous smiling at my wife" he declared. "Tomorrow I makes complaint about yous to 'ospital."

The smitten young doctor attempted to grimace at this threat but his face was totally immobilized by the Botox. Instead he slunk off into the night, wobbling precariously on his crutches.

Mail order Masha finally returned home eager to tell

Vasilis all about the prison protest he had missed and her moment of television stardom. She was brimming with excitement as the smitten young reporter planned to put her name forward as the next weather girl on the local television channel. He appreciated her ample assets could make her the next Petroula, the controversial weather girl who became infamous for reading the weather reports in a bikini. However Vasilis' earlier ardour had receded following his nocturnal encounter with the smitten young doctor and he launched into a tirade about discovering the stalking interloper in the garden.

Harsh words were exchanged as the argument between mail order Masha and that old fool Vasilis escalated, finally culminating in Vasilis announcing he was putting Masha on a tight budget and she could whistle for her cheek fillers. "I won't need yous money when I am famous weather girl, an' as for the other, consider me now on a sex strike" Masha retorted, before flouncing off to sleep in the spare bedroom.

Vasilis had a restless night. When he woke up the next morning he was still determined to limit Masha's spending money but he also realised he did not want to lose her. Blaming the smitten young doctor for their latest argument he made a phone call to the local hospital and reported the doctor was a perverted stalker. The hospital administrator decided this was the last straw as the smitten young doctor was already under investigation for surgical incompetence after botching up the reattachment of Toothless Tasos' severed fingertip. The smitten young doctor was duly relieved of his post at the hospital with a recommendation he not be rehired on the islands.

The meddling of that poor old fool Vasilis had backfired as prior to his phone call the smitten young doctor was due to return to the islands. Now he would remain in the area and without a job he would have more time to devote to stalking mail order Masha.

Mail order Masha didn't bother to greet her husband as she trotted off to the village atop Onos the donkey. She was determined to look her absolute best so she could land the weather girl job. If that old fool Vasilis would not pay for her vital cheek fillers she would find a way to have her latest surgical procedure done on the cheap. After making an appointment at the beauty parlour to have her hair extensions coloured and false nails applied she sashayed into the hard ware shop to enquire what type of filler Bald Yannis had in stock.

"This 'ere filler is good to apply in cracks so I supposes yous could use it to fill in your frown lines" Bald Yannis announced to the horror of the wrinkle free Masha.

"What about that sealant what goes round sinks?" Masha asked him.

"Well this sealant 'ere is made of silicone" Bald Yannis told her, waving round an expired tube of industrial strength bathroom sealant.

"Shouldn't think it would do any harm to yous as you 'alf made of silicone anyways."

"Just gets on with it" Masha demanded. "I make small 'ole in my cheek with this needle and you squeeze in silicone as if yous is squeezing tube of toothpaste."

"Well I will 'ave to charge extra for my services on top of price of sealant and needle" Bald Yannis stated, wiping his hands on the oily chainsaw rag before proceeding.

Mail order Masha's cheeks blew up like two rigid golf balls and the weight of them prevented her opening her mouth and speaking in anything more than a hiss.

"'Ows I going to announce weather like this?" she hissed, but Bald Yannis just shrugged as he couldn't make sense of her pathetic spluttering. He hadn't any more time to waste on this air-headed woman's vanity as he had an important date to keep with the matchmaker.

Chapter 31: Stolen Breakfast

Quentin and Deirdre were determined not to let the sound of Achilles the borrowed builder's hammering detract from their enjoyment of an alfresco breakfast in the 'Lemoni Spiti' garden. The pair had strolled along to Rapanaki carrying a small camping stove and a saucepan. Quentin had braved the chicken coop to retrieve four newly laid eggs which Deirdre duly boiled. They were just sitting down to their breakfast of soft boiled eggs and fresh figs when Fotini put in an appearance from over the garden wall and rudely snatched the eggs from their eggcups.

Achilles was dragged down from his ladder to translate. "She says you promised 'er eggs for looking after chickens."

"Well yes, she is welcome to any surfeit of eggs, but not the very eggs from our eggcups" Quentin stated. He was interrupted by the arrival of Fotini's new parrot attaching itself to his head and screeching "gormless Quentin steals eggs from old ladies."

"I am not stealing Fotini's eggs" Quentin shouted, getting into a pointless argument with the parrot. "The hens are mine and while Fotini is quite welcome to any excess eggs she has not got a right to take them all."

"She seems to think she has" Deirdre said, grabbing Quentin's arm and pointing to a sign pinned up on the entrance to Fotini's garden reading 'Fresh Eggs for Sale.' "The brazen old woman appears to be selling our eggs for her personal profit."

"Oh I see the parrot has taken a liking to you son" Hattie cried, scrambling nimbly over the garden wall to join them.

"Surely you don't begrudge Fotini a few eggs after all the trouble she has been to looking after your livestock. Have you any idea what is happening to Nitsa as we haven't heard any news since her last interview with Amnesty International and poor Fotini is quite distraught over the fate of her cousin?"

Quentin promised to make enquiries in the village regarding the current prison situation of Nitsa. However as he stood up to leave it suddenly proved quite impossible to remove the parrot from his head as its claws were firmly implanted in his scalp.

"I'm not walking back to Astakos with this parrot stuck on my head" Quentin declared.

"We must find some way to entice it off" Deirdre agreed, thinking her husband had never looked less elegant.

"Try and tempt it off with a bit of that soft boiled egg" Hattie suggested.

Fotini cut the egg in two and the parrot lunged forward to snatch it in its beak. However its claws were still firmly implanted in Quentin's scalp and he pulled Quentin with him. It only released its painful hold when it had gobbled the runny egg, causing Quentin to fall flat on his face. Fixing the parrot with a steely eye from his position prostrate on the ground Quentin surveyed its now yolky beak and said "at least someone got breakfast today."

Deirdre helped Quentin up and brushed him down, ushering him back towards their neglected al fresco breakfast table. "Enough is enough" Quentin declared "we have tolerated Fotini clambering over the garden wall in a rude and intrusive fashion for far too long. Why can't she simply walk through the gate like a normal person?"

"I have an idea to put paid to her trespassing" Deirdre volunteered. "We could plant some prickly pears on our side of the garden wall and the barbed spikes are sure to protect our privacy. Those prickly plants grow high very quickly and I hear the fruit is most delicious and would make an excellent addition to our outdoor breakfasts."

Planting a kiss on Deirdre's face Quentin praised her. "What an ingenious wife you are. We should definitely pay a visit to the garden centre and purchase some prickly plants, though I am not sure how much of a deterrent they will be to that deplorable parrot."

Chapter 32: High Spirits And A Goosing

Slick Socrates, in his capacity as Nitsa's lawyer, had been called to a meeting at the prison to discuss her case with the prosecutor and no less a person of importance than the actual government Minister for Prisons. The government was attempting to weather the embarrassment of Nitsa's incarceration which had prompted an international clamouring of concern. The illustrious minister was all for releasing Nitsa immediately, eager to wash his hands of the problem, but the prosecutor was emphatically insisting Nitsa stood trial for her awful crimes.

"Minister you fail to understand the gravity of this old lady's offences" the prosecutor argued. "She has caused grievous bodily harm to an employee of the electric company and it could be months before he is released from the hospital."

"I see your point" the minister replied, mulling over the predicament in his mind, "as obviously the government values the block vote of the electric company employees. Nevertheless the fact is concerned citizens from many countries are bombarding the government with demands to have this frail old lady released. The Japanese are being particularly strident after their citizens were gassed by the local police and we really cannot afford the bad publicity Amnesty International is stoking up."

"Criminals must pay for their crimes even if their cases become hot political footballs" the prosecutor insisted.

"'Ave you no compassion?" Slick Socrates questioned. "We are talking about a little old lady who does not deserve to be behind bars."

"I'm inclined to agree with you Socrate" the minister said. "It really makes the Greek government look callous to incarcerate an old lady while the whole world looks on. With the huge number of cases awaiting trial because of the endless judiciary strikes this could be backlogged for years. We could release her on compassionate bail and by the time her trial is called she could well be dead as she is already well past eighty."

The three men continued to argue over Nitsa until finally a decision was made. Nitsa was summoned to the governor's office to hear their verdict. The news they intended to release her until her trial date, which would be at some point in the next decade, did not receive the reaction they expected as they had no idea how much Nitsa was enjoying milking all the attention.

"Of course we will have to impound your Mercedes taxi" the prosecutor told her. This represented his only victory in the proceedings.

"You may as well keep me locked up then if I can't 'ave my taxi" Nitsa declared emphatically. "'Ows I suppose to get round without my wheels? Fotini's 'ouse would be as much a prison as my cell 'ere if I can't 'ave my taxi back. I'm not going nowheres without my taxi so yous may as well take me back to my cell."

"But surely you would rather be free than suffer the horrendous torture you have been claiming to endure?" the prosecutor asked sarcastically.

"It not my fault the public are so gullible they fall for my tall tales" Nitsa said, wishing they would get a move on. She was planning to make a small fortune on the prison black market by selling the contents of the many exotically stamped care parcels she had received and wanted to get back to her eager and captive punters. She had no intention of being released until she had flogged off the last of the international goodies.

She intended to sample the sake the Japanese prime minister had sent her but sell on the mescal tequilla that had arrived from Mexico as she thought the worm floating around in the clear yet potent liquid was quite disgusting.

She had no intention of leaving the prison confines until she had amassed a huge profit on the Cuban cigars sent by Castro and the calvados the French ambassador to Greece had donated. She was pleased her pleas for strong spirits had been heeded as she had stressed in her interviews that they were the best thing to keep dangerous prison germs at bay.

"Guard, take her back to her cell until we have discussed the matter of the Mercedes taxi further and can reach a consensus" the prison minister said in exasperation. If he didn't have to deal with the officious jobs worth of a prosecutor he would have been happy to personally drive Nitsa home in her taxi as he relished the prospect of attaining international fame as her saviour. He was furious that the press conference he had scheduled earlier in anticipation of announcing Nitsa's release would now need to go ahead with no satisfactory outcome negotiated.

Back in her cell Nitsa engaged in a brisk trade of contraband, stuffing the money in her bloomers for safekeeping. She was less than delighted when she broke a tooth on the hidden file Fotini had baked into the homemade cake she had sent in. She wasted no time in placing a telephone call from her illicit mobile phone to the young reporter at the local news station. She told him the prosecutor had punched her in the mouth causing one of her few remaining teeth to fall out.

The cameras zoomed in on the prison minister as he held the press conference outside the prison gates. "I am diligently working on freeing Kyria Nitsa" he announced "but some legal technicalities remain which must be sorted out first."

The young reporter interrupted the prison minister, demanding to know if there was any truth to the allegation the prosecutor had smacked Nitsa in the mouth, causing her to lose a tooth.

"Certainly not, that is an outrageous lie concocted by a

spiteful old woman" the prosecutor butted in.

"Then how do you account for this?" the young reported demanded to know, holding aloft a photograph of Nitsa with a gawping blood stained mouth and the missing tooth held between two gnarled fingers.

"No more questions at this time" the prison minister shouted. "I hope to have the matter resolved within the hour."

Ushering the prosecutor back onto the prison grounds the minister told him unless he was prepared to agree to the release of Nitsa and her taxi he would personally see to it that the prosecutor was prosecuted for his violent action of hitting a defenceless old lady and he would be locked up in prison until his trial.

"But you know I never laid a finger on her and this is nothing short of blackmail" the prosecutor huffed.

"You can call my bluff or you can do what is right for the good of our country" the minister said. "This whole situation is an international embarrassment and I won't tolerate your stubbornness one moment longer. Guard, bring the troublesome old crone back to the office and I will sign her immediate pardon on compassionate grounds."

By the time Nitsa was returned to the governor's office her bloomers were positively rustling, stuffed as they were with copious bank notes. Having cleaned up all the ready cash in the prison she was ready to be released. Sensing the tension between the prosecutor and the prison minister she decided to try her luck and demanded monetary compensation for her time behind bars. "Don't push your luck or I will change my mind" the prison minister told her. "I am letting you go home and you can keep your blasted taxi. All charges will be dropped on condition you stop talking to the press after we make a joint statement during which you thank me for my benevolent intervention."

"Po po you drives an 'ard bargain. Let me just put some

lippy on before we face camera together" she told him, undoing the top button of her hideous old lady dress in preparation for a bout of provocative posing.

The pair of them received international television coverage when the prison minister announced Nitsa had been pardoned of all charges. His hope that his televised appearance would improve his chances of becoming the next prime minister were dashed when he watched the footage which showed him brandishing an enormous lipstick imprint from the passionate kiss Nitsa subjected him to while goosing his bottom.

Chapter 33: Bald Yannis Finds A Wife

The matchmaker greeted Bald Yannis and Tall Thomas in the high mountain village and introduced them to the crude farmer who was willing to offer a dowry in exchange for offloading his daughters. Insisting he have the exclusive first pick Bald Yannis entered the farmhouse, leaving Tall Thomas twiddling his thumbs outside.

The four sisters were sat in their Sunday best waiting to be inspected by Bald Yannis. Three of the daughters were quite comely, though the effects of hard labour had taken an obvious toll on their looks. The fourth sister, Soula, was least noticeable as she was evidently subdued. She was used to being ignored due to her stunted growth, her abject plainness and her obvious lameness, which was the unfortunate result of a close encounter with an ill-placed bear trap.

Bald Yannis took in the pitifully poor surroundings. The very basic farmhouse was dark and airless, with religious icons offering the only decorative touches on the mould stained walls. The rooms lacked any comfortable furnishings and boasted no needless luxuries such as a television or washing machine. He thought the outdoor bathroom must be an uninviting prospect on cold winter nights. Bald Yannis shuddered as he realised even his hardware shop was more homely than this hideously bleak house.

He avoided eye contact with the three daughters who were desperate to make a good impression in the hope of escaping their hard and boring backwater situation. They hoped to hook themselves what the matchmaker had described as a 'prosperous businessman' who lived in an idyllic village by the sea. Although Bald Yannis did not exactly look like a catch he was preferable to some of the ancient and vulgar men they had been paraded in front of in past meetings, and his village was far enough away to sever the stultifying bonds with their father. They could not hide their desperation to be married and feared even if this rich suitor chose them their father would scare him off before the deal was agreed as he was notorious for failing to keep his nasty side concealed.

The fourth daughter Soula was so used to being overlooked she did not even attempt to be so bold as to try and catch Bald Yannis' eye. She presumed her lot would be to stay on the shelf while her more presentable sisters were chosen and married off. Bald Yannis indicated he would like to speak to the father privately outside. "'Appen I coulds take short one off yous hands for enough goats" he offered.

The father was most surprised by this turn of events and immediately tried to sell off one of his other daughters, proclaiming, "Soula is best worker of lot and I'd be reluctant to parts with 'er. Wouldnt's you rather 'ave one of prettier ones than plain, lame Soula?"

Bald Yannis had been terrified at the sight of the three pretty predatory sisters and had no intention of taking any of them as his wife as they scared the living daylights out of him. There was something about Soula though that made him feel protective and he told the farmer she was the only one he would contemplate marrying. "Let me speaks with 'er alone while you shows others off to Tall Thomas" he suggested.

Soula limped her way outside to join Bald Yannis, craning her head to take a look at her bald suitor. The docile look in her eyes reminded Bald Yannis of his darling pet goat Agapimeni and it lessened the trepidation he felt about initiating a conversation with an unknown woman.

"It's a bit bleak up 'ere" he began "must be a bit desolate in winter."

"It's all I've ever known" Soula replied. "I 'ere you live by sea, that must be a wonder to see."

"You means yous never seen sea?" Bald Yannis questioned.

"Father don't believe in making unnecessary treks away

from village when there's work to do. I is good worker, can scrub and look after goats, pick olives and cook" she told him, remembering her father had instructed his daughters to sell themselves as hard workers.

"Does you like goats then?" Bald Yannis asked her.

"I is very fond of goats but 'ate to cook 'em and won't eat 'em" Soula confessed, revealing a gentle stubbornness.

"I is vegetarian with a pet goat so if you marries me you never 'ave to cooks goat" Bald Yannis promised. "You'd 'ave to clean 'ouse and 'ardware shop and it would 'elp if you is a dab 'and with a chainsaw."

"Chainsaw is like third 'arm to me" Soula told him. "I cuts all wood for 'ouse. I mights be little but I is super strong."

"Does you thinks we could rub along as 'usband and wife then?" Bald Yannis asked.

This most unromantic of proposals was actually the kindest words Soula had ever heard as it offered her the means of escaping her tyrant of a father. "I reckon we can" she replied "but father said you would only be looking at my prettier sisters."

"Po po looks is overrated" Bald Yannis declared "strong is better. Should I tell matchmaker to go aheads and makes it legal?"

"Yes please" Soula told him breathlessly, fearing at any moment her new found dreams of living by the sea could be dashed by her brutal father.

Just then Tall Thomas came striding out of the house in a terrible temper having almost come to blows with the father who had unleashed his repugnant side.

"Let's get out of 'ere Yanni. There's no way on earth I am becoming entangled with this family" he bellowed. "I don't care how bigly the dowry is, it isn't worth being related to that throwback who is more of a jailer than a father."

The stricken look on Soula's face alarmed Bald Yannis, making him determined not to leave her in the clutches of a man who may well change his mind about parting with her. Striding back into the house he negotiated firmly with the father, securing Soula's immediate release on the understanding she would stay at the house of the matchmaker until their wedding. He had to agree to forgo fifty of the promised goats and to send the father a brand new chainsaw in exchange for his daughter's hand in marriage.

Taking his leave from his new fiancée Bald Yannis said "I will sees yous at wedding then."

He was taken by surprise when Soula stretched up to plant a soft kiss on his cheek, reminding him of Agapimeni's wet nuzzling. "I looks forward to being yous wife" Soula told him with gratitude as he really could not imagine how dreadful her life had been in the high mountain village.

"Yous is brave man to take on spawn of that devil" Tall Thomas said to Bald Yannis as the pair drove away. "I 'ad 'eard on village gossip vine he was 'orrible man with reputation for violence but no one mocks my 'onest business of fish selling with such contempt as he did. I tells you Yanni I nearly punched 'im even though he is pensioner. I feels sorry for 'is daughters but they ooze desperation which is not an attractive trait. If yous is marrying short one I dont's wants to tell you all bigoted things he said in case it puts you off 'er."

"Soula is not 'er father and I don't plans to 'ave anything to do with 'im" Bald Yannis said. "He agreed to keep away from Soula in exchange for a new chainsaw and he is not invited to wedding. Matchmaker is fixing it up for Soula and I to marry in Dimarcheio later in week and I'd be mightily pleased if you'd agree to be my koumbara."

"Well I'd be 'appy to do that for yous if you don't think Moronic Mitsos will be too insulted" Tall Thomas told him. "In meantime I think I'lls forget about getting wife until I see 'ow you gets on with married life."

Chapter 34: Buoyant Times For Botox

The villagers were all busily embroiled in preparations for the upcoming panagyri. Prosperous Pedros had been persuaded to dust off and play his bazouki, while Quentin and Deirdre were enjoying impromptu Greek dancing lessons from Fat Christos. Considering how obese he had been before his recent weight loss Fat Christos was remarkably nimble on his feet and his enthusiasm was contagious.

"Stop dancing and strumming" Stavroula called out in annoyance. "Yous needs to get out to sea and catch us some lobsters. Toothless Tasos hasn't managed to catch a single one and it will be a pretty poor show if our lobster festival 'as no lobsters."

"Well Gorgeous Yiorgos 'as always been the king of lobster catching" Fat Christos said, "but we'll get the boats out and give 'im a 'and."

"What's she trying to 'ide under her 'air?" Prosperous Pedros queried as they passed mail order Masha attempting to look inconspicuous with her long hair extensions combed over her face.

Mail order Masha was desperately looking for the smitten young doctor to see if he could apply any damage control to her two blown out cheeks. The pressure from the solidified bathroom sealant silicone was excruciatingly painful as it had hardened like concrete. Spying the doctor hobbling into the beauty parlour on crutches Masha tottered after him as fast as her ridiculously high heels could carry her.

Having been unceremoniously sacked from his job at the hospital the smitten young doctor was desperately seeking new career options. Despite austerity wracking Greece the market for Botox had never been so buoyant and the doctor wanted to discuss the possibility of opening a Botox clinic in the curtained off back room of Evangelia's beauty shop.

"Well I can let you rent the space behind curtain for your

Botox clinic, but I wouldn't think there's much demand for it in village. There's only Masha who is vain enough to want toxic poison injections. You would need to be in big city to find enough paying customers to make any money" Evanglia told him.

She was interrupted by the arrival of mail order Masha. Masha was still unable to speak in anything beyond a hiss so she was forced to endure the angry tirade the smitten young doctor directed at her. "Your husband has not only had me sacked from my job with his ludicrous complaints about me stalking you, but he also assaulted my broken foot with a humongously heavy watermelon."

His anger mellowed when he realised Masha was unable to respond with anything more than a splutter, while desperately jabbing her fingers in her cheeks to attract his attention to their unnatural state.

"Good grief Masha, what has happened to your beautiful face?" he questioned in sudden sympathy. He looked perplexed as she attempted to hiss the words "bathroom sealant."

"There there, don't try to speak, I think you are possibly in need of medical attention" the doctor said.

"Well you're a sacked doctor not a struck off quack" Evangelia interjected, "do something to help her, the poor darling is in obvious pain."

The smitten young doctor instructed Evangelia to run across to the supermarket for a bag of frozen peas to help reduce the swelling. She returned in a jiffy with the bag of peas and with Masha's good friend Tassia, who held Masha's hand as the doctor set to work extracting the hardened silicone lumps from her face, using his Botox syringe as a make-do anaesthetic.

Masha was able to speak once again as her face deflated. She explained her husband had turned into a skinflint and she had resorted to desperate measure to obtain cheek fillers so she would look her absolute best in her interview for the position of weather girl with the local television channel.

"It's not Bald Yannis' fault" she admitted, "I begged him to do it. 'Ow was I supposed to know I would end up looking so revolting? Now the television station will never hire me and I can't even get pregnant as I am on a sex strike to punish that old fool Vasilis."

Tassia led Masha over to Stavroula's taverna and settled her down with a large glass of vodka, assuring her the smitten young reporter would still champion her dream to be the next scantily clad weather girl. "Your face will look normal in a day or two, and everyone is still talking about how smashing you looked on the television at the prison protest."

"'Ow are things with Fat Christos?" Masha asked, with genuine concern for her friend.

"Everything is wonderful apart from his interfering mother hinting the baby's not his" Tassia confided. "I'm quite tempted to get the nasty secret out in the open and tell Christos who the real father is. I know Christos will stand by me but I am terrified if word gets out the real father will make demands."

Tassia suddenly clammed up at the sight of Slick Socrates taking a seat at a nearby table. Mail order Masha noticed the sudden blush on her friend's face and a hideous suspicion suddenly dawned within her. She had a passing thought that Tassia's baby would be born sporting Socrates' trademark sideburns, before discarding her sudden worry as quite preposterous.

Chapter 35: The Mystery Of The Knee-Length Underpants

Thea was doing her best to avoid Toothless Tasos, certain he would be enraged her debts had once again got the better of her. She decided to try and rent out the harbour-side house again, but would need to advertise it as unfurnished as the debt collectors had cleaned the place out. She was surprised the fastidious widow Mrs Christeas had left the house with a trail of rooster feathers leading from the kitchen to the bedroom, and set to sweeping them up. Discovering a pair of men's grubby knee-length underpants in a dusty corner of the bedroom led her to tut with disapproval, but her mind was too preoccupied with monetary worries to give more than a passing thought to whom they could possibly belong to.

Meanwhile Stavroula was angry enough to spit feathers as she made the discovery that one of her new roosters was missing. She immediately placed a telephone call to the man who trained guard dogs and stressed her need for a ferocious beast was urgent. He promised to deliver a well trained guard dog by the end of the week, leaving Stavroula's remaining roosters woefully unprotected in the meantime.

Returning home for lunch the Pappas was dismayed to find Mrs Christeas serving up the remnants of the previous evening's rooster in red sauce with macaroni. "Is this only thing you can cooks woman?" he asked her, thinking Petula had at least served up a more varied diet.

"I thoughts yous like rooster" Mrs Christeas wailed.

"I do, but not for three meals every day" the Pappas complained. "'Ow about a nice bit of fish for dinner tonight?"

"'Ow about you takes me out to eat at taverna instead of expecting me to cooks?" Mrs Christeas demanded.

"Knows your place woman, yous is 'ousekeeper and if I takes you out people will gossip."

"'Ousekeeper with benefits" she pointed out, patting her ample bosom to distract the Pappas and attempting to calm him by stroking his chin with a rooster feather.

The Pappas was in no mood to be played. He launched into a litany of criticisms, telling the amorous widow she had rather slovenly habits for a housekeeper and comparing her lacklustre attempts at keeping a clean house with the industrious standards of the departed Petula. Deciding to forgo the left over rooster dish in favour of a cheese pie from the bakery he stomped out after demanding she clean up all the feathers.

Mrs Christeas was left worrying her position as the Pappas' housekeeper could well be imperilled so she set about cleaning the house with a vengeance. Sweeping up all the loose feathers she pondered the possibility of sewing them onto her bra as a tickling embellishment to tempt her lover, but gave up on the idea when the feathers proved a bit itchy. Swatting a pesky fly away she had the novel idea of sewing all the feathers together to create a unique fly curtain to hang up in the kitchen doorway. After several hours of meticulous needlework her fly curtain was taking shape nicely until she ran out of feathers and decided it was time to go out and steal another rooster.

When Toothless Tasos returned home from a fruitless morning out at sea attempting to catch evasive lobsters he was delighted to discover Thea had prepared an appetizing yet frugal lunch of fasolada and bread. Thea offered Tasos a heartfelt apology for allowing her debts to run out of control and assured him she hoped to find a new tenant for the harbour-side house very soon.

"I 'ave taken on extra knitting from Mrs Kolokotonis and will stick to a strict budget. I never wants to 'ave to hide from debt collectors again and I promise to start watching the cents. We can saves some money if we eats fish what you catches instead of meat."

Toothless Tasos took Thea into his arms, reassuring her he would not leave her if she was sincere about mending her spendthrift ways.

Hoping to make Toothless Tasos laugh Thea waved the knee-length pair of grubby men's underpants under his nose, telling him "look what I found in widow's bedroom. I'm dying to know who they belongs to."

Staring at the out-dated underwear Toothless Tasos quipped "for ones moment I thoughts yous been buying more 'orrible rubbish off 'ome shopping channel. You don't thinks widow is elusive underwear thief does you?"

"Underwear thief only stole women's under things" Thea said, dismissing the suggestion. "I thinks stuck ups widow 'as been entertaining a man in 'er bed. I should have charged 'er double rent."

"If yous is right she'll 'ave to stop doing that now she is living under roof of Pappas as 'ousekeeper. The Pappas won't stands for any goings on under 'is roof'" Toothless Tasos said naively, adding "still it does makes you wonder who widow 'as been 'aving in 'er bed."

The two of them shared a smile. Toothless Tasos wondered how long Thea would keep him out of her bedroom, while in turn she wondered if she wasn't being a bit hard on him. If even the awful Mrs Christeas was having a love life perhaps she ought to consider welcoming Tasos into her bed. They were as good as married and he was proving to be a rock to rely on amidst her financial crisis.

Chapter 36: Oily Trees

"I 'opes you is not offended I asked Tall Thomas to be koumbara at wedding" Bald Yannis said to Moronic Mitsos, thinking he perhaps should have asked Mitsos to take on the role to keep him on side for his 'catfisher' scam.

"I is not offended at all" said Mitsos who hated weddings and wouldn't now need to waste any of his generous police pension on a present, as he wasn't invited.

"'As the English teacher successfully bribed border guards to get out of that hell hole African pit?" Moronic Mitsos asked Bald Yannis.

"She is working on it" Yannis lied, reminding himself to transfer the moron's money for the generous non-existent bribe into a separate bank account. "It is 'ard to believe but she says you is 'andsome, manly and most impressive specimen. 'Ow do yous 'opes to 'ide 'er from your wife when she lands up in Greece?"

"I suppose I will 'ave to send wife off to 'ave 'oliday with son on island" Moronic Mitsos said, beginning to have second thoughts. This whole business of attracting a foreign floozy was proving a most costly venture and he realised it might stretch the imagination of any but the most gullible woman to accept his leaky rowing boat was an actual yacht.

Taking his leave from the hardware shop Mitsos said "Kalimera K-Went-In and Did-Rees" to the American pair entering the store.

"We are planting some prickly pear plants against our garden wall and hope you sell protective gardening gloves to make the task less painful" Quentin announced.

"Theys is 'orrible plants and could do someone agonizing damage" Bald Yannis replied.

"Well we have decided to plant them as a deterrent to stop Fotini and Nitsa climbing into our garden without an invitation" Deirdre told him.

"Did yous know Did-Rees this type of prickly cacti is often planted to ward off evil eye 'an them two old crones 'ave definitely got evil touch? 'Appen you'd be better off with landmines and a moat against that gruesome twosome" Bald Yannis suggested, wondering if he could source some landmines from his black market contacts.

Slamming a pair of protective gardening gloves on the counter Bald Yannis asked, "K-Went-In, 'ow many 'ours does you make Did-Rees work in 'ouse?"

Quentin looked askance at this question and replied "I do not make Deirdre work; we are a partnership and share the chores between us."

Bald Yannis was rather baffled by this response. He considered the whole point of acquiring a wife was to put her to work. "I didn't have yous down as one of them new fangled feminists" Bald Yannis said, shaking his head at the strange habits of foreigners. Comparing Deirdre to the Greek women of his acquaintance he realised she was a pampered creature. Stavroula was not afraid of hard work at the taverna and old Mrs Kolokotonis was forever knitting in her attempts to succeed as an entrepreneur, in addition to serving in the supermarket.

"Seeing you share chores you'll be needin' an extra pair of protective gardening gloves" he declared, slamming a second pair down on the counter and laughing raucously at the sudden image he had of Deirdre struggling with a large hardy frankosyko plant. At the same time he imagined how easily Soula would take such a difficult and prickly plant in her stride and warmed to the idea of tying the knot with her. Not wanting to be drawn into a long unnecessary conversation Bald Yannis picked up his chainsaw, revved up the motor, and scooping up the cat announced "time for this one to 'ave its 'aircut."

Deirdre fled from the shop so quickly she almost fell over the Japanese tourists who were hoping to snap more selfies with the pet goat Agapimeni. Bald Yannis had been mulling over another way to scam these polite tourists. The olive trees he was about to take ownership of as part of Soula's dowry were sorry looking specimens, hardly producing enough oil to warrant collecting the olives and putting in the back breaking work of pruning. He hoped to ensnare the Japanese tourists into sponsoring an olive tree each. In return he would promise to send an annual photograph of their tree and a small bottle of olive oil. He need not bother trekking up to the high mountain village to take pictures as he intended to fob them off with a photograph of a random tree, as one olive tree looked much like another to the untrained eye.

One of the Japanese spoke excellent English and was able to negotiate with Bald Yannis on behalf of the tourist group. "We think it would be a wonderful idea to sponsor oily trees if you promise to send photographs and name the trees after each sponsor. My name is Takeshi which means unbending. I would be honoured to sponsor an unbending tree that is eulogised with my name."

Bald Yannis painstakingly wrote the name Takeshi in his ledger, closely followed by the Japanese names for child of calmness, tortoise child, multiple accomplishments, happy generations, bright boy, fourth born son and a thousand storks. After much conferring Takeshi pointed to one of his party and announced "his name is Matsu which means pine tree and he wants to sponsor a pine tree instead of an oily one."

"Okay, tell him I will give him a bottle of retsina instead of olive oil" Bald Yannis capitulated while scooping up their cash. "Like taking candy from a baby" he muttered under his breath, quite shocked they had so easily parted with one hundred Euros each for the promise of having a tree named after them.

"We tell all our friends in Japan so they can do sponsorship business with you over the internet" Takeshi said while bowing. "It makes us happy to help your beautiful country in this way."

"If you're interested you could sponsor a goat each as well" Bald Yannis volunteered, remembering he was about to take ownership of fifty new goats as part of Soula's dowry.

After conferring once again with his group Takeshi expressed their total approval of this latest sponsorship scheme, provided Bald Yannis dressed each of the sponsored goats in unique knitted clothes.

"You'll 'ave to pay extra for knitted goats clothes" Bald Yannis told them and was for once gobsmacked as they emptied their wallets so readily. He realised the goat sponsorship scheme would require a herd of goats all dressed in clothes. It would take more organisation than his random tree scam and each individual goat would need to wear a Japanese name tag. Luckily he had arranged for the dowry goats to be delivered to Astakos and Soula would soon be on hand to lovingly tend them. He hoped she was a dab hand at knitting as Mrs Koloktonis was about to be snowed under.

It struck him as a pity that he needed to spend good money on these clothes when he could have dressed the goats in the stolen underwear still stashed in his house. He realised he would be on dodgy ground though if Stavroula and Thea recognised their stolen knickers being modelled by goats.

Chapter 37: Spiked By A Prickly Pear

"I needs a stiff drink" Prosperous Pedros announced, taking a seat in 'Mono Ellinka Trofima' that evening.

"'Ave a vodka" mail order Masha suggested "it is made from potatoes so is vegetarian."

"I'll stick with wine from Greek grapes" Prosperous Pedros said, shuddering inwardly at the thought of needlessly sampling anything foreign.

"Nitsa is back at my mother's 'ouse and 'as been bending my ear for 'ours with 'er ridiculous tales of life in prison. There we all was protesting for 'er release an' she was 'aving time of 'er life drinking brandy and eating takeaways. Can you believe the scheming old crone even made a small fortune flogging off illicit liquor sent to 'er from gullible foreign governments?"

"My aunt is a crafty one all right" Tall Thomas laughed, relieved the old dear was no longer incarcerated behind bars. "'Appen I should take her on in my mobile fish business as she don't miss a trick and is a bit of a celebrity now."

"What 'appened to you two?" Yiota asked Quentin and Deirdre as they entered the taverna sporting painful looking scratches all over their arms and faces.

"We have been wrestling with some rather large and unwieldy frankosyko plants all afternoon" Quentin replied.

"Yes mother 'as spent the last hour complaining about yous planting them prickly pears" Prosperous Pedros piped up "let me buy you a drink as I think you 'ave got the better of 'er and that's not easily done."

"Well it's not that we are trying to be unneighbourly but we really would prefer it if your mother did not continually scramble off her three-legged olive ladder and over our garden wall, invading our privacy" Deirdre explained.

"Ow is 'ouse coming along?" Takis asked them.

"Achilles the borrowed builder is making quick progress

and the house will be habitable in no time at all" Quentin replied.

"Does you all knows Bald Yannis is to be wed tomorrow?" Tall Thomas asked.

"We were in his shop this morning and he never mentioned it" Deirdre said, looking surprised.

"We had no idea at all he was even courting and he certainly didn't ask us to the wedding" she added, feeling slighted as they had reluctantly invited Bald Yannis to their leaving party earlier in the year.

"He didn't do no courting, he got 'er through match maker" Tall Thomas told her. "It not a wedding in church with big ceremony, they will just sign register in office in Dimarcheio. 'Appen if you turn up at noon to pay your water rates bill you will see it all as cashier doubles up as registrar."

"I think we can survive without witnessing some poor woman getting lumbered with Bald Yannis for life" Quentin stated, to the annoyance of Deirdre who was eager to see what type of woman would agree to marry the lunatic from the hardware store. She would love nothing more than to gatecrash Bald Yannis' wedding.

Gorgeous Yiorgos entered the taverna swinging a grey mullet by its tail. "Yiota can you cooks up this fish with a nice lemon dress whilst I telephone Petula to come 'ere to join me?" he asked. "I am worn out, I been out in boat since dawn and 'not 'ad sight of a single lobster. Did yous 'ave any luck Pedro?"

"Not a single one" Prosperous Pedros replied. "Things is looking pretty dire for the lobster festival as no one 'as caught one yet. At this rate all we'll 'ave for panagyri is sardines."

"I'm thinking them pilfering fishermen from Gavros 'ave been sneaking into our waters and potting all our rightful lobsters" Tall Thomas opined. "I reckons the slimy chap with mobile fishing van from Gavros will turn up on day of festival and try to sell us our own lobsters."

"Well we wont's buy 'em" Takis declared, adding "'ow dares they sneaks into our waters and poaches our lobsters. Sardines will do us well enough if needs must."

"My mother's offer of Idaho potato ice-cream still stands" Quentin said to the obvious disgust of everyone present.

Slick Socrates entered the taverna, having been sent round by Stavroula to see if any other villagers were missing their roosters. "Stavroula is in a right state" he announced "she is now missing four of her prime roosters and 'as convinced 'erself the elusive underwear thief as taken to stealing birds."

This shocking news caused quite a stir in the taverna as no one wanted to think there was once again a thief in their midst. Quentin said "I think all our roosters are tucked up in the brand new chicken coop, but I didn't actually count them."

"I'll telephone mother for yous and ask 'er to pop round and do a quick comb count" Prosperous Pedros offered, whipping out his mobile phone.

"I never eat rooster as I find it too tough and tasteless" mail order Masha said, emphatically ruling herself out as the rooster thief. She wouldn't put it past her step-daughter Stavroula to accuse her and couldn't help but notice Slick Socrates gaze was fixated upon her silicone chest.

"You wouldn't 'ave a clue 'ow to cooks it anyways" that old fool Vasilis said, adding "everyone knows yous can't cooks anything but borscht."

"I'm still dying to taste your infamous borscht" Deirdre told Masha, to which she replied "yous can sample it at panagyri. I'll cooks up a big pot and bring it along as it's likely we'll starve if we depends on this useless lot to catch lobsters."

Yiota emerged from the kitchen carrying the platter

of grey mullet in a lemon dress. Gorgeous Yiorgos asked Quentin, Deirdre and Prosperous Pedros to join him as Petula had decided to stay at home and keep a watchful eye over their hens and roosters. "Petula is really worried if someone is stealing roosters they might not stop there and it would break 'er 'eart if anyone made off with 'er goat Nero."

"Stavroula is getting a vicious guard dog to protect 'er birds" Slick Socrates told the room at large while still staring at mail order Masha's silicone chest "but she won't sleeps easy now until it is chained up in yard."

Prosperous Pedros was just about to tuck into his fish when his mobile phone demanded his attention. "'Ow could she forget about spikes when she 'as been complaining about 'em all evening" he shouted into the phone. "Why can't she just use the path like a normal person?"

Standing up to take his leave he announced Fotini had forgotten all about the prickly pear bushes that had been planted against the neighbouring garden wall and had fallen headlong into them when clambering over the wall to take a head count of Quentin's roosters. "Nitsa says mother is impaled on a prickly pear plant and is stuck full of spikes like a pin cushion. She can't haul her up as she's too 'eavy for Nitsa and Hattie so I 'ave to go over an' pull 'er out of plant an' see if she needs go 'ospital."

Blanching a ghostly shade of white a rather guilty Quentin stood up and offered to drive Prosperous Pedros to Rapanaki to assist him in hauling Fotini out of the bushes.

"I fear we'll never hear the last of this" he whispered to Deirdre.

Chapter 38: Fotini Is Rescued From Impalement

Quentin and Prosperous Pedros were nearly deafened by Fotini's agonised screams when they arrived at the house. Fotini had fallen flat on her back with her skirt all askew, revealing her bloomers. Her hideous old lady dress was thoroughly impaled on the razor sharp spikes of the over sized prickly pear plant. Short of stripping it off she had no way of disentangling herself from the spiky embrace of the enveloping bush. Every attempt Nitsa and Hattie had made to free her left her even more intertwined, with the barbed skewers of the plant cutting painfully into her skin. To complete the ridiculous picture the parrot had taken up permanent residence on top of her head.

"Mother hold still 'an shut up yous screaming, we is 'ere to rescue you from grip of plant" Prosperous Pedros called out.

"Who that you got with yous?" Fotini wailed.

"It's that malaka Quentin what is responsible for your plight" Nitsa told her, frantically trying to rearrange Fotini's skirt so Quentin would not be overcome by lust at the sight of her bloomers.

"Quentin, this is all your fault" his mother Hattie admonished him.

Quentin felt the accusation was unjust and leapt to his own defence, declaring "I had every right to plant prickly pear plants in my own garden and if Fotini had just used the path like any normal person this would not have happened."

"Quentin you cannot blame the victim. Fotini was simply taking a well established shortcut in order to take a head count of your roosters. Stop being so full of righteous indignation and get over here and yank her out of the bush" Hattie commanded.

"'An' keep your eyes off my bloomers you malaka" Fotini shouted, almost drowned out by the parrot screeching

"Quentin likes women's bloomers."

With much hauling and heaving the two men were finally able to extricate Fotini from her impalement on the vicious prickly pear plant. Nitsa had passed them open ended tin cans to protect their hands, a tried and tested means of tackling the fruit without being stabbed by hairy thorns. They sat Fotini down on top of the garden wall where she sat swigging medicinal brandy from the bottle and wailing "my dress is ruined."

"We can get yous a new dress from 'ardware shop in the morning" Nitsa reassured her, welcoming any excuse to get close to Bald Yannis.

"Yes, and Quentin will pay for it, won't you dear?" Hattie added.

"Of course, and I will also pay for Fotini to have her hair untangled in the beauty parlour" Quentin agreed, staring at the many pear needles protruding from Fotini's bird nest styled mess of hair, giving him a sudden appreciation of the phrase 'looking like you've been dragged through a hedge backwards.'

"'Ardware shop mights not be open for yous to gets new hideous old lady dress as Bald Yannis is getting wed tomorrow" Prosperous Pedros piped up.

"What? It can't be true. Does you mean to say Bald Yannis 'as found 'imself another woman while I was locked up in ghastly prison? I'm not 'aving this, he 'ad 'is eye on me an' I not 'aving some other woman steal 'im" Nitsa yelled in a fit of jealousy, demanding to know who the floozy was who had stolen her man.

"He went to a matchmaker for a wife" Prosperous Pedros explained. "Are you seriously saying Bald Yannis 'as been trifling with your affections and leading yous on cousin Nitsa? He wouldnt's even join protest to 'ave you released from prison an' calls yous despicable."

"Po po, it's all in 'er imagination that Bald Yannis 'as is

eye on 'er" Fotini interjected. "Nitsa fancies 'im but there were never no sign he reciprocated."

"What about time he couldn't take 'is eyes off me in 'ardware shop" Nitsa said.

"Well I 'ates to tell you but it was 'ard to take eyes off that false eyelash that was stuck to yous lip like a moustache" Fotini shouted. "He 'as turned down your body every time you 'ave thrown yourself at 'im, admit it."

"There must be something wrong with 'im. What red-bloodied man could resist me? Matchmaker must 'ave found 'im a real beauty if he prefer 'er to me" Nitsa insisted.

"Yous is deluded" Fotini argued, annoyed she was no longer the centre of attention. "Yous is old enough to be Bald Yannis' granny."

Fed up of listening to the old crones bickering Prosperous Pedros offered to carry his mother back to her house. Hoisting her up in a fireman's life he looked over his shoulder and suggested Nitsa and Hattie do something to remove the parrot which had inserted its claws into Quentin's scalp and was perched ridiculously on his head.

Chapter 39: Botoxed Old Crone

Adonis was delighted when the contingent of Japanese tourists asked if they could stay an extra two nights in his hotel. They had heard on the village gossip vine their good friend with the darling goat from the hardware shop was getting married and wanted to go along to pay their respects and wish him well. Adonis had not managed to con any of them into buying a house but was happy to hear they fully intended to return to Astakos for future holidays to visit the goats they had sponsored. Bald Yannis had successfully negotiated the use of one of Moronic Mitsos' fields as the new home for the dowry goats. The moron was delighted the goats would keep the weeds down and save him the expensive bother of employing a man with a strimmer.

"You must all come along to the village panagyri where we eat lobster and dance to the bouzouki" Adonis invited.

Accompanied by Fotini and Hattie, Nitsa was standing in the hardware shop doorway waiting for it to open, hoping Bald Yannis would be so entranced by her beauty he would call off his wedding. She was most put out when Moronic Mitsos opened the shop, explaining Bald Yannis was busy making the newly arrived dowry goats feel at home in his field. "We needs three new dresses" Nitsa demanded.

"Yous mean these hideous things?" Mitsos enquired, pointing at the dusty and drab shapeless button-up dresses suspended on coat hangers from the ceiling.

"I don't think I need a new dress" Hattie said, not wanting to tell her new friends she wouldn't be caught dead in such a hideous frock.

Grabbing the dresses Nitsa said they wouldn't bother to try them on as there was no opportunity for her to flash Bald Yannis with a bit of her temptingly exposed bosom. "We dont's want to be late for our appointment at beauty parlour" she said, dragging her friends along with her.

Mail order Masha was most put out to discover the quiet morning she had planned at the beauty parlour in anticipation for her interview as the local television station's weather girl was to be disturbed by the three noxious old bags demanding blue rinses and lip waxes. Nitsa had managed to persuade Fotini and Hattie to gatecrash Bald Yannis' wedding with her and she planned to pull out all the stops with a full makeover. Fotini had been easily persuaded as she loved nothing more than a good wedding and couldn't wait to spit all over the bride.

"What on earth have you done to your 'air" Evangelia asked Fotini, surveying the unruly mop stuffed full of prickly pear spikes and wondering how she could extricate them without hurting her fingers.

"Don't asks" Fotini replied, trying to block out the humiliating memories of the preceding evening.

"Ladies may I interest you in my new service of Botox injections to remove all your wrinkles" the smitten young doctor asked, emerging from behind the curtain.

"Whos you calling wrinkly?" Fotini asked "you young 'ens should learns some manners."

"I'll gives it a go" Nitsa volunteered, adding "desperate times call for desperate measures an' this 'ere Botox mights take years off me."

"Yous go down that route and you mights ends up looking like mail order bride 'ere" Fotini scoffed, looking disapprovingly at Masha.

"Chance would be a fine thing" Masha retorted, knowing she looked her silicone best since the problem with her concrete cheeks had been resolved.

"What exactly is in that needle" Hattie asked the smitten young doctor as he injected Nitsa.

"It is simply a shot of botulinum toxin intended to paralyse the facial muscles" the doctor said airily.

"So Nitsa could well come down with botulism, a

potentially deadly form of food poisoning" Hattie persisted.

"Only thing likely to give me food poisoning is that disgusting potato ice cream of yous" Nitsa fired back.

"Oh no, he can't sees me like this" Nitsa suddenly screamed, fleeing behind the curtain. She had spotted Bald Yannis about to enter the beauty parlour and did not want him to catch her with wet blue gloop all over her head and a line of hair removal cream over her moustache.

"Can I leaves Agapimeni here for wash and blow dry before wedding?" Bald Yannis asked. He wanted to make sure his pet goat looked her best when he introduced her to Soula.

"I cans squeeze yous in too" Evangelia offered, thinking his botched hair transplant was in desperate need of a tidy-up.

"Po po no need to make a fuss, wedding will be done and dusted in five minutes" Bald Yannis replied. With only Tall Thomas due to turn up at the registrar's office he didn't even plan to go home and change out of his work clothes. He was sure Soula was a sensible girl who would take him as she found him.

Checking her appearance in the mirror mail order Masha realised she would outshine any bride in the beauty department. Turning to the old crones she said "as you ladies are off to the wedding 'ave you room for one more in your taxi if I rush home to change?"

"As longs as yous can pay extortionate taxi fare yous is welcome to comes along" Nitsa replied, convinced by the time Evangelia had finished pampering her she would far outshine the plastic Masha and the interloper of a bride.

Chapter 40: Mid-Morning Kleftiko

Quentin and Deirdre, enjoying coffee at Stavroula's taverna, were engaged in a rare argument. Having learnt the Dimarcheio was a public building Deirdre really wanted to turn up to satisfy her curiosity about Bald Yannis' wedding. It was no use Quentin pointing out they had not been invited as she responded they did not need an invitation to pay their water rates.

"Quentin the bill needs paying anyway. It will simply appear circumstantial if we turn up at the exact moment the dreadful hardware man ties the knot in the same office where the bill must be paid. You must admit it will be amusing and it will keep you well away from the house. I'm sure you want to avoid Fotini after last night's terrible debacle."

Quentin conceded his wife had a point. Even though he was sure Fotini would be resting up in bed after her painful experience of yesterday evening, rather than hovering around on the garden wall, he didn't want to give the parrot another chance to implant its claws into his still delicate scalp. Nevertheless he remained convinced it was bad form to turn up uninvited at the wedding.

Stavroula stomped over to their table announcing "kokkoras" whilst flapping her arms aloft to indicate a bird was gone. Attempting to answer Stavroula in Greek Quentin queried "kleftiko?" confusing the word with 'kleftis,' the correct word for thief. Stavroula flounced back to the kitchen, thinking how self absorbed the Americans were. She had expected sympathy over the theft of her roosters but all these foreigners could think of was their stomachs. Marching back over to their table she slammed down two plates of kleftiko, a traditional Greek dish of lamb cooked slowly in parchment.

"It looks as though you mixed up your Greek again" Deirdre said in exasperation as they had only just finished their breakfast. "Look, kleftiko is even on the menu. What were you trying to say to Stavroula?"

"Thief" Quentin responded, realising even if he had got the word right it may well have come out sounding all wrong if Stavroula had misinterpreted the word as an accusation rather than a question.

Catching the sympathetic eye of Gorgeous Yiorgos Deirdre asked him if would mind awfully asking Stavroula to put the kleftiko into a take-out package for them to eat at the beach after the wedding.

"That reminds me I promised to drive Petula and Thea to Dimarcheio as they loves a good wedding. 'Appen as you twos is going up to pays your water rates bill you coulds drive the ladies up and saves me the 'assle. I really oughts to be gettin' back out at sea looking for lobsters for panagyri" Gorgeous Yiorgos said. Backed into a corner Quentin had no choice but to agree to go to Bald Yannis' wedding with the trio of ladies.

Chapter 41: The Bride-To-Be

As the morning of her wedding to Bald Yannis dawned Soula was almost giddy with excitement, yet remarkably free of any pre-wedding jitters. Although she had only met her husband-to-be for a brief moment she had formed a pleasant impression of him as a firm and hard working man. She was naturally worried that he may find her lacking in sophistication as she had led a very hard life in the high mountain village with her tyrannical father. Still, Yannis had struck her as a down to earth, pragmatic businessman, who seemed happy enough to take her as he found her.

During the several days she had stayed at the home of the matchmaker she had never been exposed to such luxury. She had a room of own in contrast to being crammed in with her three sisters in one room decked out with two sets of bunk beds. She had been intrigued by the new fangled television and had taken a guilty pleasure in watching the soap opera 'Seven Deadly Mothers-in-Law'. It was a relief not to have to step outside to perform her ablutions in the outdoor bathroom, but nothing quite compared to the heady feeling of being free from the constant work demands of her father.

Now she was about to be married, something she never imagined would happen to her before her three prettier sisters. She had presumed she would serve as a lifelong drudge until the moment her father kicked the bucket. Even if such a fortuitous event were to occur she had presumed she would live out her days in the depressingly bleak farmhouse in the remote mountain village.

Soula had never had any time to take care of her appearance. The mirrors in the matchmaker's house were quite a revelation, reflecting her plain guile free face, staring back. The matchmaker had insisted on taking Soula along to have her hair cut and the hairdresser had set to with a pair of tweezers to divide her overgrown monobrow into two distinct eyebrows. Soula would have liked to buy a pretty dress for the wedding, but her father had never given her any cash for such frivolities so she was resigned to getting married in her serviceable work dress.

She found it hard to believe that by the end of the day she would be a married woman with a home of her own in a beautiful seaside village and vowed to be the best wife she could to Bald Yannis as she was filled with gratitude towards him.

When the matchmaker told her it was time to leave for the Dimarcheio Soula had a skip in her step for the first time ever.

Chapter 42 Porridge and Unplucked Roosters

"I 'ere that ungodly Bald Yannis from 'ardware shop is getting wed by registrar today" Mrs Christeas told the Pappas, serving up watery porridge for his breakfast.

Staring at the bowlful of unappetizing slop the Pappas complained, "I don't know what world's coming to when peoples dont's get married in church. A good wedding would 'ave 'elped fill up church pews. Mind yous no one can stands Bald Yannis and I bets none of people he 'as invited will turn up at 'is wedding. Who's he marrying anyway, I 'ad no idea he was courting?"

"I 'eard he got wife from matchmaker" Mrs Christeas said.

"Meddling matchmakers were responsible for landing me with the ungrateful Petula" the Pappas confided. "'An look 'ow she turned out, nothing but a floozy."

"It is terrible the way she left you for another man" the widow agreed, being totally ignorant of the Pappas' reputation as a drunken wife beater. "Why dont's you turn up at Dimarcheio? With a bit of God bothering you mights persuade 'em to change plans and get married in church in proper Godly fashion."

"I mights just do that" the Pappas concurred, opening the fridge door to see if there was any yoghurt to thicken his porridge.

"What's that awful stink?" he demanded to know, just as his eyes clapped sight on the as yet unplucked decapitated rooster sitting on a silver platter in the fridge. "Ow many times does I 'ave to tell you I ams sick to death of eating malaka roosters" the Pappas swore.

"But I plan to concoct a totally new dish from this one and 'ave stuck its body in the fridge as it makes feathers easier to sew on fly curtain."

"Yous not going to cook it up with red sauce and macaroni

then?" the Pappas questioned.

"I was going to roast it as a treat" the widow told him, convinced in her mind that rooster was a much needed aphrodisiac. The Pappas appeared to be losing interest in her ample charms and she was desperate to keep his attention. Luckily he had no interest in where she was acquiring so many roosters and knew there was no way the meagre amount of housekeeping money he doled out would stretch to such luxuries unless she stole them.

Realising there was no hope for the porridge the Pappas stormed out of the house without a word. He decided to take the widow's advice and create a God-bothering scene at the Dimarcheio, but first he intended to exercise his legal right to have his weekly visitation with the pet goat Nero. He hoped Gorgeous Yiorgos would not be at home as he never failed to whip out the photograph of the Pappas and Mrs Christeas doing unspeakable things on the kitchen table and mocking his grubby knee-length underpants.

Chapter 43: What A Darling Bridesmaid

Kyria Ananas had endured a tedious morning in her office at the Dimarcheio where she doubled up as both the cashier and the registrar. Annoyed there was no time to nip out for a quick cigarette before the scheduled noon wedding she shuffled a precariously perched pile of dusty paper files across her desk, making room for the marriage register. She expected the formalities to take no more than five minutes as the paperwork all seemed in order and the only people expected were the bride and groom, the koumbara and the matchmaker.

She was completely taken by surprise with the arrival of a large group of Japanese tourists dressed formally in black suits and colourful kimonos, asking if they were in the right place for their good friend Yannis' wedding. There was barely room to fit them all into the pokey office so Kyria Ananas immediately began shoving all the surplus chairs into the corridor. Bald Yannis, arriving next with Tall Thomas, was taken aback to find such a large audience, but could hardly tell them to clear off when he had so carefully nurtured their business.

"What are yous doings 'ere" he questioned Quentin, Deirdre, Petula and Thea as they squeezed their way into the tiny office.

"We are here to pay our water rates bill" Deirdre replied, quite shocked that Bald Yannis had not bothered to dress up for the occasion.

"Bride is 'ere" Tall Thomas whispered to Yannis, spotting Soula and the matchmaker being unceremoniously shoved aside by the gaggle of old crones, Fotini, Nitsa and Hattie, with mail order Masha trailing behind them.

"Where's my rival then?" Nitsa demanded to know, peering round and failing to spot a likely candidate.

Bald Yannis ignored her as he went to greet Soula, telling

her he would try to get rid of all these unwelcome and uninivited interlopers. Soula assured him she didn't mind the throng of well wishers, thinking she was so lucky to be marrying such an obviously popular man.

"Ang on a minute, I wants you to meet Agapimeni" Bald Yannis said to Soula "I'll just run outs an' brings 'er in."

Mail order Masha watched this exchange with interest, realising the short plain lame woman dressed in a serviceable dress was the bride. Rushing over to her she whispered "surely you dont's want to get married in that ugly frock?"

"Of course not but I 'ave nothing else" Soula confided.

"I 'ave spare dress in my bag because after wedding I needs to get changed for job interview at television channel, but I looks so gorgeous in this one so you can borrow spare. Yous is a bit flat chested but if I pins in the back it should fits you nicely" Masha kindly offered, dragging Soula towards the ladies room to get changed.

"You can't bring goat in 'ere" Kyria Ananas said as Bald Yannis led Agapimeni into the office. The goat was beautifully dressed in a lime green knitted dress with a matching fascinator.

"My darling is staying" Bald Yannis insisted "she is bridesmaid."

The Japanese tourists were in their element snapping selfies with the goat dressed as a bridesmaid. Bald Yannis was so distracted wondering where his bride had disappeared to, he failed, for once, to charge the requisite fee for pictures of his goat.

"You looks almost pretty in my dress" mail order Masha complimented Soula, rubbing blusher into the bride's cheeks. Soula had never even imagined such a stunning dress, let alone worn one. Masha was so leggy her lavender mini dress was a respectable knee-length on Soula and the sparking Swarovski crystals adorning the plunging neckline reflected the glimmer of excitement in the eager bride's eyes.

"'Ere you'd best stuff some toilet paper in yous bra" Masha commanded, standing back to survey her handiwork. Satisfied her impromptu makeover made the bride almost passable she said "Bald Yannis won't knows what 'as 'it 'im.""

Relieved his bride-to-be had not done a hasty runner through the toilet window Bald Yannis rushed to her side to introduce Agapimeni. "Oh she looks so lovely in dress an' 'at" Soula proclaimed, prompting Bald Yannis to say "you looks nice too."

"Shalls we gets started?" Bald Yannis asked Kyria Ananas, to which she replied "'old your 'orses, can't you sees I am seeing to water rates business."

The delay was fortuitous for the Pappas, arriving just in time to voice his strenuous objections to a civil, rather than church ceremony. Tripping over the bridesmaid's lead he landed in an unruly heap on Deirdre's feet, shouting "proper place for wedding is in church yous ungodly heathens."

Cameras went into overdrive as the Japanese tourists snapped photos of the prostrate Pappas being kicked by the goat. Dragging himself to his feet the Pappas continued "there is no dignity to office wedding without all churchly formality and no one to ask if anyone knows any lawful reason why yous two cannot be joined in legal wedlock."

"I objects" Nitsa screeched "it should be me what Bald Yannis is marrying."

Spotting the sudden confusion on the face of the bride Deirdre instructed Quentin "oh for goodness sake, get that deluded old bat out of here before she ruins everything."

"That's no way to talks about my old aunty" Tall Thomas objected.

"Well yous aunt and Pappas are determined to ruin a perfectly good wedding and needs removing" Thea piped up.

"Best get rid of this old hag too before she starts spitting all over my dress" mail order Masha added, pointing at Fotini.

The unbending Takeshi and Child of Calmness rushed to help Quentin frogmarch Nitsa and Fotini out of the building. To everyone's surprise the bride found her voice, telling the Pappas "I've no truck with yous religion and sees you is nothing but a God-bothering fraud. Now gets out so I can marry my man."

Even though they had no idea what Soula had said the remaining Japanese tourists burst into spontaneous applause and Tall Thomas roused himself enough to physically eject the Pappas. Kyria Ananas announced they had best get started as she was desperate to dash outside for a cigarette break.

Five minutes later all the formalities were completed and Bald Yannis and Soula were legally married. "You can kiss bride" Kyria Ananas said to the horror of Bald Yannis who had never in his life kissed a woman. Sensing his embarrassment Soula took the initiative and planted a kiss on the goat bridesmaid. In keeping with their traditional wedding customs the Japanese all burst into hysterical crying and pressed 'Goshugi Bukuru', gaudy money envelopes stuffed full of Euros, onto the newlywed couple.

"These are a bit brighter than usual brown envelopes we 'ave 'ere" Kyria Ananas hinted, hoping in vain the groom would slip her a back hander.

Chapter 44: The Weather Is Sunny

The smitten young reporter was illegally parked on the pavement outside the Dimarcheio, waiting to whisk mail order Masha off to her interview for the job as weather girl at the television station in Paraliakos. "You looks irresistible" he told her as she slid into the car wearing an off-the-shoulder green velvet evening dress with a high-thigh side slit.

"I 'ad pink mini dress to change into but gave it to bride as she looked a fright, and I looks gorgeous whatevers I wear" Masha confided while plucking donkey hairs from her bosom and removing the smitten young reporter's roving hands from her legs.

"I really thinks this job can make me as famous as Petroula Kostido" Masha said.

"You is much more voluptuous than 'er" the smitten young reporter declared "but yous will 'ave to wear more clothes than she did in front of cameras. Dids you knows the television station what employed 'er got smacked with a massive fine when watchdog agency ESR was flooded with 'undreds of complaints her near nakedness did not meet the necessary qualitative standards?"

"I dont's needs to strip off to showcase my curvaceous figure" Masha said adjusting her neckline to reveal more silicone cleavage. "I 'opes the job comes with a generous clothing allowance as that fool of 'an 'usband of mine 'as padlocked 'is wallet."

"As longs as yous can talks knowledgeable about weather, job is sure to be yours" the smitten young reported assured her.

Prising her eyes away from her compact mirror Masha glanced outside, pronouncing "today it is sunny."

"There you goes, yous is natural" her admirer declared.

Chapter 45: Mopping And Blushing

"Woulds you likes see my 'ardware shop now" Bald Yannis asked his new bride, trying to pull her away from the suffocating embraces of all the uninvited guests still milling around outside the Dimarcheio tossing confetti.

"That would be nice" Soula agreed.

"I liked the way you stood up to God-bothering Pappas, I 'ave no time for the nasty obsequious man" Bald Yannis told her.

"I 'am 'appy to 'ere my little outburst did not displease yous" Soula said "but I dont's like church and 'ad to say so."

Seeing Soula hesitate to enter his shop Bald Yannis asked her "yous dont's like my 'ardware shop?"

"Oh, it's not that" she rushed to reassure him "but it looks a bit filthy in shop and I dont's want to spoils this beautiful dress the nice Russian lady gave me. Let me just change out of it and I'll set to with a mop and bucket and 'ave this place clean as a pin in a jiffy."

Bald Yannis was inordinately pleased his new wife was already showing her value as a hard worker. "I'll leaves you to gets on with it then" he told her, heading off to the kafenion for a coffee."

"Whats you doing in 'ere, I 'eard you just gots married?" Prosperous Pedros asked.

"I dids just get married and now new wife is mopping 'ardware shop" Bald Yannis announced to the amazement of the other villagers.

"Yous can't treats new wife like scrubber on 'er wedding day, 'ave some respect" Gorgeous Yiorgos told him with genuine outrage.

"But she offered to set to with cleanin'" Bald Yannis said, failing to comprehend what he had done wrong.

"Womans needs fuss making of 'em on wedding day and expects an honeymoon period" Gorgeous Yiorgo schooled him. "Yous can shows 'er yours 'ardware shop, but not put 'er to work in it. 'As she even seen 'ouse where she'll be living yet?"

"Not yet" admitted Bald Yannis, realising he was a little afraid of being alone in his house with Soula, having no idea what she expected from him in the bedroom department. There was only the one bedroom and he supposed he couldn't really expect Soula to sleep on the floor.

"At least brings 'er 'ere for coffee and introduces 'er" Petros the Postman suggested, only to have his idea rebuffed when Bald Yannis said "I thinks she is shy. I'll show 'er 'ouse and yous can all meets 'er at panagyri when she's 'ad time to get used to bein' married."

Spotting Bald Yannis drinking coffee in the kafenion Nitsa rushed over, observing "yous is bored of married life already. I suppose nows you 'ave wife I'll 'ave to settle for being yous mistress."

"Keeps out of my 'air yous deluded old granny" Bald Yannis screamed in disgust, heading back to the hardware shop to relieve his new bride of her mopping duties. He could hardly believe his eyes when he saw how quickly Soula had transformed the shop from grimy to gleaming, realising she would be a real asset to his business.

"I shows you 'ouse now" he said tenderly as Soula turned her back to conceal her ready blushes.

"Does you minds if we walks slowly to 'ouse? I 'ave never seen anything as beautiful as Astakos and want to looks at everything" Soula asked.

"I 'ad never really noticed but suppose it does 'ave pleasant vista" Bald Yannis replied.

Soula vocalised her admiration for all the new things her eyes were drinking in. "Looks how lovely turquoise hued sea is lapping against 'arbour walls and all them fishing boats bobbing around so colourfully. The air is so salty fresh, with the bougainvillea almost dancing in the breeze.

Even olive trees all looks 'ealthy and fruitful."

Listening to his new wife baring her poetic soul Bald Yannis considered she could be an asset in penning fake love letters to Moronic Mitsos. It struck him there seemed no end to Soula's talents.

The pair bumped into Mrs Kolokotronis hand delivering her latest batch of knitted goat's clothes. She was delighted to hear Soula was an expert knitter. Soula willingly agreed to help out when Mrs Kolokotonis expressed the need for more hands on needles. As talk turned to the imminent panagyri Mrs Kolokotronis lamented it looked as though the lobster festival would sadly be missing any actual lobsters.

"We needs something else to make panagyri a success" she said, prompting Bald Yannis to suggest a beauty contest for goats, naturally all kitted out in knitted clothes. Soula clapped her hands in joy, proclaiming she had never known such excitement.

As the newlyweds passed the moron's field filled with the newly arrived dowry goats Bald Yannis was pleased to note they all appeared in robust health. "You 'aves nurtured 'em wells" he praised his new bride who responded "I can't wait to see 'em all dressed up in beauty pageant."

Luckily Soula didn't have a jealous bone in her body; otherwise she may have been saddened the goats were undoubtedly going to be better dressed than her.

Reaching the house Bald Yannis told Soula "we is 'ome. I 'opes you like it, it is better than what you is used to but yous is welcome to gives it some womanly touches."

Soula thought Bald Yannis' rather neglected house was a little palace compared to the bleak farm house she had escaped from. "Oh Yanni it 'as inside bathroom" she exclaimed delightedly, adding "'an' I think there will be wonderful views from windows once I've given 'em a good cleanin'."

Looking at the thin mattress lying on the living room

floor she said "even bed looks comfortable."

"That's not my bed, I means yous bed, that's where Agapimeni sleeps" Bald Yannis confusedly corrected her as he still hadn't worked out the new sleeping arrangements. Opening the door to the bedroom revealed a sparsely furnished room featuring a double bed and a chest of drawers. Hurriedly shoving an oily chainsaw under the sheets Bald Yannis explained he kept it to hand in case he needed to slice up any burglars.

"Are there burglars in village, how dreadful? I won't be frightened of 'em with you 'ere to protect me" Soula said.

"Well there's someone running round stealing roosters" Bald Yannis told her, thinking it best not to mention the elusive underwear thief who had terrorised the village until recently. Remembering his washing line exploits reminded Bald Yannis he had a gift for his new wife and he duly presented her with a brown paper wrapped package of stolen underwear.

"Oh Yanni I 'ave never seen such exquisite undies" Soula exclaimed, pressing mail order Masha's silk thong to her cheek, fingering the lace bows of Thea's bra and testing out the elasticated waist of Stavroula's knickers."

"'Ang on I don't know 'ow these got in ere" Bald Yannis said, hastily grabbing an enormous pair of Fotini's bloomers and using them to wipe oil off the chainsaw. Attempting to hide his sudden embarrassment he presented Soula with a freshly caught sea bass.

"I got us this nice fish off Tall Thomas for yous to cooks for our dinner. I'll leaves yous to sorts it out and gives 'ouse a good clean while I runs back to open up 'ardware shop for evening."

Chapter 46: Taverna Chat

That evening the locals in 'Mono Ellinka Trofima' were discussing the following night's panagryi.

"Whoever 'eard of such nonsense as a goat beauty pageant?" Prosperous Pedros asked, having heard the latest plans to liven up what was looking to be a lobsterless panagyri.

"'Well maybe Bald Yannis got idea from them rich Arabs what are always 'aving camel beauty competitions" Gorgeous Yiorgos said. "I don't thinks it's a bad idea an' Petula is 'oping for first prize for 'er pet goat Nero."

"'An Tassia can do sketches of winner and runners up as prizes" Fat Christos suggested, eager to show off his wife's prowess as an accomplished goat artist.

"Did wedding go off wells Did-Rees?" Prosperous Pedros enquired.

"Well your mother had to be forcibly ejected to stop her spitting all over the bride and your cousin Nitsa was thrown out when she objected to the marriage, declaring Bald Yannis belonged to her. The Pappas made a God-bothering fool of himself, the Japanese tourists became quite hysterical and the bridesmaid was a goat wearing a fascinator. Apart from that I think it went very well though I feel sorry for the plain little thing who is now stuck with Bald Yannis" Deirdre replied.

"I thought she scrubbed up quite nicely in mail order Masha's dress" Quentin added.

"I feels sorry for 'er as Bald Yannis 'as no idea 'ow to treat a woman" Yiota said.

"Well althoughs he's an arrogant sod he 'as been taking a bit of advice on 'ow to treat women because he admits he is clueless" Gorgeous Yiorgos said in a surprising defence of hardware shop man.

Suddenly all the fisherman sat upright and sucked in their

stomachs as mail order Masha sashayed into the taverna trailing that old fool Vasilis behind her. "I got job as weather girl with the local television channel and starts tomorrow night" she announced to a round of tumultuous applause.

"I am so 'appy about job I 'ave given up sex strike" she added, which explained why that old fool Vasilis looked so knackered. "Tomorrows I will cook up 'uge pan of borscht as I knows 'ow much you are dying to taste it Did-Rees, but I wills 'ave to leave panagryi earlys for first appearance as weather girl."

"I am indeed looking forward to finally tasting your infamous borscht" Deirdre admitted.

"Will you be cooking up one of your spit-roasted goats?" Quentin asked Yiota.

"Not unless someones is lucky enough to 'ave a bit of road kill before tomorrows" Yiota replied.

"Perhaps we should encourage Nitsa to drive around in her taxi on the off chance" Quentin quipped.

"With any luck she'll drive over smitten young doctors other foot" that old fool Vasilis giggled.

"'Ave you caughts any lobsters yet?" Masha asked the fishermen.

"Not a one" Prosperous Pedros plaintively confirmed "but I 'ave an enormous bucket full of sardines."

Mail order Masha turned her nose up in disgust at the thought of this common fare and proceeded to denounce all the gathered fishermen as completely useless.

"I am 'avings vodka in morning with Bald Yannis' new bride Soula" she announced. "I will takes 'er a bag of my old clothes as poor little thing 'asn't got anything pretty to wear. She was so grateful when I gives 'er my mini dress for wedding. I wonder if she fancies my 'old 'air extensions as well."

"You 'ave a 'eart of gold my love" that old fool Vasilis told his wife. "Even thoughs you is about to become famous weather girl you still 'aves compassion for unfortunates."

Preening with delight mail order Masha slipped an extra tab of Viagra into her husband's drink, whispering to him "if yous is on top form tonight with a bits of luck I'll be needings a whole new pregnancy wardrobe soon."

Chapter 47: Is That Even Legals?

"I can't believes you got us kicked out of wedding with your jealous carryings on" Fotini was still complaining to Nitsa the next morning. "You knows 'ow much I enjoys a good spitting on bride."

"Why did you want to spit on her?" Hattie asked Fotini, presuming Nitsa had put her up to it out of jealous malice.

"It is tradition to spit on bride to ward off evil eye" Fotini assured Hattie while desperately trying to dislodge the parrot from her head.

"She don't wants do it for tradition, she just loves covering 'em in spit 'an she knows full well brides 'ate being spat at by nasty old women" Nitsa argued.

"Well we 'ad to put up with it when we was wed" Fotini pointed out. "Didn't no one spit all over you when yous married K-Went-In's father?"

"Certainly not, mine was a respectable wedding" Hattie proclaimed.

"Wells if that Randolph boyfriend of yous ever turns up I will spits all over yous at wedding" Fotini promised with an evil cackle.

"Spits on 'Attie, spits on 'Attie" the parrot screeched.

"I've had enough of the parrot's nonsense" Hattie declared. "If anyone wants me I will be in the kitchen preparing my famous Idaho potato ice-cream for this evening's festivities."

"I don't knows why you bothers, no one will eats it" Nitsa called after her, adding "We're off for a drive in taxi."

The parrot refused to move from the top of Fotini's head so she covered it up with a tea towel hoping people would think it was a fashionable new hat. As they drove through Astakos they spotted mail order Masha sitting with Bald Yannis' bride at Stavroula's taverna.

"Nows yous chance, calls 'er over" Nitsa instructed,

slowing down to allow Fotini to spit all over Soula.

"You disgusting old bag" mail order Masha screamed at Fotini as the taxi sped away, but Soula was actually delighted to have been the victim of this obnoxious old custom, confident it would bring her good luck. "I'm glad she didn't spit all over your lovely dress yesterday but todays it don't matter as I is just wearing old rags."

"Not for much longer" Masha said, passing Soula a carrier bag full of her old sequined dresses and all the hideous old lady dresses she had received from the village women on her last birthday. "Makes sure you dress up for panagyri tonight."

Spotting the sudden tears welling up in Soula's eyes Masha asked if Bald Yannis had been treating her badly.

"I dont's knows what to do, I is confused," Soula confided. "New 'usband gives me lovely underwear as wedding present. I puts it on an' felt pretty but by time he got back from 'ardware shop it was covered in fish guts. I never 'ad to gut a fish before and made terrible mess, we only 'ad dried salt cod up in mountain village, not fish that is still slimy what you can't hold down on chopping board."

"Po po yous don't want to be gutting nasty fish, I gives you the recipe for my infamous borscht an' Bald Yannis wills love it as it is vegetarian. What 'appened next Soula, did yous consummate marriage?"

"No, I thinks sight of me in underwear covered in fish guts put 'im off and he slept in goat's bed. An' then when I was cleaning up in 'ardware shop this morning I found a love letter he had written to a man called Mitsos and I thinks I must 'ave married an 'omosexual" Soula wept.

"Wipe your eyes" Masha comforted Soula. "Everyone knows Bald Yannis 'as been writing letters to Moronic Mitsos as a joke, making 'im think they was from a foreign woman looking for an 'ansome Greek man. He used to read bits of 'em out in kafenion for a laugh. Mitsos is so moronic he fell for it, he even believed Shirley Valentine from film was real woman writing to 'im. Yous new 'usband isn't an 'omosexual but I suspicions he may well be a virgin."

"Oh what a relief" Soula cried "I is virgin too. Cans you give me some tips on 'ow to get 'im interested in me in bedroom?"

"Makes sure he drinks plenty of vodka at panagyri and then take advantage of 'is body" Masha advised, whispering some tried and tested sex tips to the virgin bride.

The by now blushing Soula asked "is that even legals?" before dissolving in laughter.

"I thinks you'll find it is" Gorgeous Yiorgos butted in. Having overheard their saucy whispering he whipped out his photograph of the Pappas demonstrating the questionable sexual position in his knee-length underpants.

"Oh my, I hopes new 'usband looks better than that without 'is clothes on" Soula said dissolving into raucous laughter.

Striding outside to see why her customers appeared to be having a good time Stavroula snatched the photograph out of Soula's hand. "Ha, God-bothering fake Pappas is having illicit relations with pious widow is he?" she spluttered with laughter.

Zooming in on every detail of the photograph Stavroula's laughter suddenly stopped abruptly when she spotted a familiar black feather sticking out of the Pappas' ear and another one wedged between the widow's pendulous breasts. Suspecting the Pappas was the rooster thief she would have loved nothing more than to hot foot it around to the church and confront him, but the taverna was filling up with Japanese tourists who all wanted feeding.

"I'll 'ave that rooster thieving malaka later" she vowed, stomping back to the kitchen.

Chapter 48: Poached Lobsters

"I 'opes you won't put me in dog 'ouse my love but I 'ave just inadvertently let out secret that yous 'usband is carrying on with amorous widow" Gorgeous Yiorgos revealed to Petula when he arrived home.

"Wells he couldn't expect to keep it secrets forever when he 'as moved 'er smugness into 'ouse with 'im. Anyways I 'ave 'eard on village gossip vine he told Bishop it was me that was 'aving affair and he 'ad to throw me out as I was disgracing 'im" Petula replied, busily polishing Nero's horns so they would gleam in the goat beauty pageant that evening.

"Nothing lost as he 'as already signed divorce papers and he deserves to pay for all them black eyes he gaves yous" Gorgeous Yiorgos said, squeezing Petula's hand.

Meanwhile the enraged Stavroula decided to persuade her step-mother to case the Pappas' house to see if there was any evidence to support her suspicions he was stealing her roosters.

"I is busy woman with no times to go sneaking rounds" mail order Masha told her. "I 'ave big pan of borscht to cooks up and tonight I starts new job as weather girl."

"It's 'ardly out of your ways at all as you pass Pappas' 'ouse on yous way 'ome" Stavroula insisted, cursing the Japanese tourists for ordering so many plates of octopus in vinegar, keeping her tied to the kitchen when there was vital snooping to do.

Climbing onto the donkey Masha headed home, making a quick stop at the Pappas' house to appease her step-daughter. Pulling out her mobile phone she reported back to Stavroula there was no one at home and no evidence of any illicit roosters. She failed to make the connection between the stolen birds and the stinking fly curtain concocted out of feathers hanging over the kitchen door, attracting a veritable swarm of flies like a magnet. Masha simply dismissed it as another sign of the Pappas' deplorable taste, but what could else one expect from a man who spent his life prancing round in a shapeless black dress.

Having enjoyed her chat with mail order Masha, Soula wandered back to the hardware shop, gushing about Masha's generosity as she showed her new husband the bag of second hand clothes. Recognising the old lady dresses as shop stock items Bald Yannis hastily shoved aside the shop soiled dress he had planned to give to Soula, realising Masha's parcel had saved him some money. He was gratified to hear Soula heaping praise on the hideous old lady dresses as most of the recipients did nothing but complain how hideous they were when they received them as gifts from their useless men folk.

The newlyweds were distracted by bellowing emanating from the harbour. "Clears off you lobster poaching swindler" Tall Thomas was yelling at the man from Gavros, who had turned up in his mobile refrigerated fish van hoping to sell Astakostan lobsters to the villagers of Astakos for their lobster festival.

"This is war" declared Prosperous Pedros "yous Gavros fishermen 'ave depleted our waters of our rightful lobsters."

"You dont's own sea" the man from Gavros shouted back breathlessly, running back to his van to avoid being pelted with sardines by the angry villagers.

"Waste not wants not" Fotini muttered, picking up the discarded sardines and wiping them on the tea towel covering the parrot stuck on her head who was repetitively squawking "this is war."

"I bets we can extort some exorbitant taxi fares by driving them Japanese tourists to panagyri in taxi later" Nitsa told Fotini.

"But panagyri is 'ere on side of 'arbour" Fotini pointed out.

"Yes but theys dont's know that an' we can fleece 'em bigly by driving round in circles" Nitsa suggested.

Mail order Masha's telephone call had not convinced Stavroula the Pappas was an innocent party in the case of her stolen roosters. She was too busy to keep popping outside to do a cock head count and was worried yet another rooster may be purloined before the ferocious guard dog arrived. When Quentin and Deirdre arrived for lunch with Adonis, Stavroula had a light bulb moment and explaining her predicament to Adonis, asked him to translate.

"She is convinced the Pappas is the elusive rooster thief and wants yous to makes room in yous new chicken coop for 'er 'ens and roosters for safe keeping until new vicious guard dog is delivered" Adonis explained.

"But we were just about to order lunch" Deirdre complained, confirming Stavroula's opinion the only thing the American pair thought of was their stomachs.

"I suppose it wouldn't take very long to transport Stavroula's livestock over to the 'Lemoni Spiti' in the car and lock them up safely in our coop" Quentin volunteered, fearful Stavroula's seething anger was about to explode in their direction.

"Well I suppose it is in a good cause if even birds are not safe from the odious Pappas" Deirdre finally agreed, never one to hide her loathing of the foot bothering churchman.

As Adonis and Quentin loaded the livestock into the car the parrot finally released its hold on Fotini, spying Quentin as a better target and sinking its sharp claws into his scalp.

"Does you want to borrow this so yous won't look so stupids?" Fotini offered, throwing the smelly sardine smeared tea towel over Quentin's head before he had time to object.

"K-Went-In yous looks less gormless in that fashionable 'at" Nitsa informed him as the two men drove off with their livestock load.

Just then the savage guard dog was finally delivered. "Oh wells chains it up outside by chicken coop" Stavroula instructed "and I'll get 'ens and roosters back in morning. I don't wan't to gets K-Went-In's back up by making 'im run round on superfluous errands."

"A pity you didn't think of that before you expected Quentin to go without his lunch" admonished Deirdre.

Stavroula gave her a filthy look before flouncing back to the kitchen, muttering "I's never met people such obsessed with their stomachs than them malaka Americans."

Chapter 49: Magnificent Physiques

The Pappas was beginning to regret so hastily inviting the amorous widow to live under his roof. Her cooking left a lot to be desired, her housekeeping skills were slovenly and she was far too demanding in the bedroom. He had no idea how anyone was expected to perform position ninety-two in her sex manual without giving himself a hernia. Fortunately he remained blissfully unaware the indecent photograph of the two of them was doing the rounds or that Stavroula suspected he was a rooster thief.

Picking up a Bible he copied down some quotations about the immorality of devilish dancing leading to wanton promiscuity he intended to deliver at the panagyri. He didn't see why the villagers should have a good time when he was so miserable. He was still smarting over the humiliation of being physically ejected from Bald Yannis' wedding and the mortification of the Japanese tourists posting photographs of him with his dress in the air when he tripped over the bridesmaid's lead, on social media. The only bright spot on his horizon was the anticipation of the goat Nero taking first prize in the beauty pageant and the vague hope the Bishop would offer him a promotion in recognition of all his invaluable work in the community.

The Pappas was not the only one making preparations for the panagyri. That old fool Vasilis was pouring generous measures of vodka into mail order Masha's simmering pan of borscht and Bald Yannis was dusting off his supply of lobster adorned shower curtains to flog that evening in a clever scheme to offer at least one type of lobster to the festivities, even if they weren't edible.

Quentin called in at the beauty parlour to see if the smitten young doctor could do anything to remove the parrot from his head. Its claws were so deeply embedded in his scalp the doctor advised nothing short of surgical removal would do the trick unless the parrot flew off of its own volition. Deirdre suggested they try to tempt the parrot off with a bit of soft boiled egg as it worked previously.

Thea was nagging Toothless Tasos to take her to the panagyri, pointing out free sardines would not break the bank and they deserved a night out. "Of course we will go to the village festival my little baklava" Tasos assured her "does you really thinks I woulds be so 'eartless to makes you stay at 'ome with yous knitting whens everyone else is partying?"

Fat Christos spotted Bald Yannis piling up lobster adorned shower curtains on a table next to the outdoor grill and demanded half of the table surface to display his tourist tat. Bald Yannis, arguing he made claim to the table first, was flashing his chainsaw around in a threatening manner. However he was shamed into sharing the table when Soula pointed out he didn't need the whole thing to display his wares as each unique lobster adorned shower curtain was identical.

"Exactly, seen one and yous seen 'em all" Fat Christos bellowed, putting his collection of glow-in-the dark Parthenons and wind-up Greek dancing dolls on the table.

"Cover up them naked statues" Stavroula screeched disapprovingly, only to be contradicted by Soula saying "there is nothing shameful about the nakedness of the Greek Gods of our heritage. They 'ave magnificent physiques we should celebrate."

Bald Yannis sucked his stomach in, hoping his new wife did not expect him to reveal a magnificent physique as he was sadly lacking in the six-pack department. Leaving Soula to rush home to get changed into one of mail order Masha's cast off sequin dresses Bald Yannis headed to the kafenion to take advice from the village men who were more experienced than him in the ways of women.

"Ow quickly does you think I can share bed with 'er

considering we is practical strangers?" Bald Yannis asked the coffee drinking men.

"Wells yous is married so yous should 'ave shared marital bed last night" Vangellis the chemist stated.

"I was thinkings of it but when I got 'ome from ardware shop she were covered in fish guts an' smelt none too pleasant" Bald Yannis explained.

"I thinks you 'ave to be sensitive and gives 'er time" Toothless Tasos opined. "Thea 'asn't let me in bedroom yet, but we's not married."

"Petula and me share bed 'an we's not wed yet" Gorgeous Yiorgos boasted.

"Yes but yous two is in love and you can 'ardly expect Soula to be in love with Bald Yannis" Petros the postman piped up.

"If yous is worried about getting 'ers pregnant I sells prophylactics in pharmacy an' if yous is worried yous can't perform I sells Viagra" Vangelis the chemist tittered.

"I not worried, just wondering if it seemly to be expecting new wife to wants to get up close and personal with near stranger so soon" Bald Yannis insisted.

"Wells Masha says new wife was crying because you slept in goat's bed rather than with 'er. She suspicioned yous was 'omosexual but Masha tolds her yous was'nt."

"I'm most grateful to yous wife for putting Soula straight" Bald Yannis sighed in relief.

"Well she told 'er yous was straight but also told 'er yous is virgin" Vasilis said to Bald Yannis' horror.

"Of course I'ms not virgin, I is over fifty" Yannis scoffed, blushing bright red and storming out of the kafenion to the mocking cries of that old fool Vasilis calling out "does goat count as willing partner?"

Seething with humiliation Bald Yannis rushed home after Soula, determined to consummate his marriage.

Chapter 50: The Lobsterless Lobster Festival

By the time the blushing newlyweds returned to the village grinning from ear to ear the panagyri was in full swing. Prosperous Pedros was playing the bazouki and the tasty smell of grilled sardines permeated the air. Spotting Takeshi attempting a few tenuous steps of Zorba's dance Bald Yannis joked "yous is not so unbending afters all."

Soula rushed over to thank mail order Masha for the sparkly sequin dress she was wearing and confided Bald Yannis would no longer be sleeping in the goat's bed. Deirdre was delighted to finally receive a large bowlful of mail order Masha's infamous borscht, declaring "it's not at all what I expected" as she wandered away to find a plant to water with the noxious brew. "Avoid the borscht" she advised Quentin "it tastes as though Masha cooked it up in a vodka distillery and is indescribably disgusting."

It was too late for Quentin to heed her advice as Masha was bearing down on him with a soup ladle, saying "you'd better sample my superior soup now K-Went-In as I must leave for my first television appearance as the weather girl and am taking the rest of borscht with me to makes good impression on my new co-workers."

Quentin attempted to tempt the parrot off his head by offering it the borscht but the bird refused it, parroting "silicone Russian cooks disgusting borscht."

Slick Socrates was busy setting up the giant outdoor television screen so all the villagers could watch Masha's first televised weather report. "She'll be on the air in another 'our" he announced to everyone's excitement as all the villagers could not wait to see if she would become as famous as Petroula.

"We'd best do goat beauty pageant now" Slick Socrates announced to the annoyance of the Pappas who had hoped to get his God- bothering sermon of doom in before the competition. "Ow many goats are competing?"

Bald Yannis pushed Agapimeni to the fore. His pet goat looked quite delightful in pink and white striped footless knitted stockings and a matching dress. Petula led Nero to join Yannis' goat and the Japanese tourists rounded up their namesakes.

"Agapimeni is so lovely she is sure to take first prize" Soula whispered to Bald Yannis, even though the goats she had reared were also competing under Japanese name tags.

The goats were paraded up and down to the amusement of the villagers who thought the spectacle most ridiculous, though the Japanese tourists loved it. When Slick Socrates announced the winner was indeed Agapimeni the Pappas screamed out that the votes were rigged and Bald Yannis had bribed the judges.

"Yous is such a poor loser for a God-botherer what is supposed to be humbles" Soula scornfully told him. Takeshi congratulated Bald Yannis and assured him it was no surprise that the most famous goat in the world should win first prize for her beauty. However his offer to purchase Bald Yannis' pet goat for an astronomical sum and sneak it back to Japan in his suitcase was flatly turned down by Bald Yannis' proclaiming "I wills never part with my darling," earning him a soft kiss on the cheek from Soula.

Nitsa and Fotini pulled up in the old Mercedes taxi, releasing the central locking once the last of the straggling Japanese tourists had been extorted of the exorbitant fare. Nitsa and Fotini had been arguing nonstop since the moment they left home as Fotini was adamant she had forgotten something vital but was having one of her senior moments and couldn't remember what it was she had forgotten. Nitsa insisted if she couldn't remember it couldn't be important. Hattie was also complaining, as she climbed out of the taxi, moaning "Why did you have to drive around for so long? I told you my potato ice cream was melting."

"Looks like it melted all over backsides of them Japanese tourists" Nitsa cackled manically pointing to the melted mess embellishing the back of A Thousand Stork's kimono. Agapimeni wandered over to lick the ice cream from the kimono to the horror of Fotini who had a mortal fear of goats and ran to lock herself in the taxi. Once she was safely ensconced she remembered the vitally important thing she had forgotten and beckoning Nitsa over she lowered the window a crack to whisper "I forgots to lock door on K-Went-In's hen 'ouse."

"Wells I'm not driving backs and roosters most likely asleep. It's time to party" Nitsa replied, rushing off to find a bottle of brandy and Bald Yannis to torment.

Bald Yannis was doing a roaring trade in lobster adorned shower curtains; convincing all the visitors to the village they had hundreds of innovative uses. "Yous can use 'em as picnic blankets or useful room dividers, as winter rugs or coffin liners" he told his captive audience while menacingly polishing his chainsaw.

"Dont's forgets they make great rain coats and is transparent to show off undies if yous remember" Nitsa simpered, brushing up against the hardware man.

"Keeps yous 'ands of my 'usband" Soula hissed "or yous be using one of them orrid curtains as coffin liner sooner than yous thinks."

"Po po I's not after yous 'usband, I 'ave man of my owns" Nitsa scoffed, delightedly spotting the handsome young prison guard with a thick moustache and a full head of hair who had refused to strip search her and making a beeline for him. Sidling up to him she announced "yous not on duty now so there's nothing to stop yous gettin' yous 'ands in my bloomers."

"Yous wants lockin' up yous deluded old hag" the horrified guard grunted, pushing her rudely aside.

The widow Christeas, not at all conspicuous by her

absence from the panagyri, was sitting at home worrying she was losing her hold on the Pappas. She disapproved of the frivolity the villagers were enjoying but realised the festival offered a risk free moment to go on another rooster stealing spree. She had convinced herself Stavroula did not deserve such prize birds as she was ungodly and never had a good word to say about the esteemed Pappas. Moreover she was convinced if she could just perfect a rooster dish to the same exalted standard as the one she had first produced to seduce the Pappas he would stop his sneering and realise she was an indispensible part of his life.

Just to be on the safe side the widow threw on one of the Pappas' old clerical dresses. The dark robes offered a suitable disguise that would not be easy to spot in the darkness. Arming herself with an olive sack in which to deposit the plundered bird she set off on her mission to steal, promising herself if it resulted in the perfect dish she would knock her pilfering activities on the head.

Her plans were thwarted when the ferocious guard dog standing guard over Stavroula's chicken coop attacked her, pinning her to the ground, sinking its fangs into the clerical dress and taking a large bite out of her bottom. Her resultant screams caused Stavroula to come running, followed by the other villagers.

"Yous thieving Pappas, I gots you now, trying to make off with my roosters. I knew it was yous" Stavroula shrieked.

"Pappas is stood right 'ere you stupid woman" Slick Socrates told her "it not 'im on floor in mouth of dog."

"Wells who is it then?" Stavroula queried, calling the dog off to reveal the widow Christeas. "Yous, yous stuck up widow what thinks yous is better than us, is thief. Socrate take 'er over to Pancratius, she deserve locking up."

"I 'ad no idea my 'ousekeeper was thief" the Pappas loudly declared, washing his hands of her fate.

"Well if yous pays up for all roosters she 'as stolen

'appen police won't involves you" Stavroula demanded. "No doubts yous been eating 'er plundered booty even if yous not steal it youself."

"Dont's let this spoil yous fun of evening" Toothless Tasos consoled Stavroula. "'An' at least I 'eard you give all roosters an' hens over to K-Went-In for safe keepin.'"

Stavroula agreed to return to the festivities, happy at least that the identity of the rooster thief was now known. She wouldn't have been so complacent if she knew Fotini had left the door to Quentin's chicken coop open and at that very moment a gang of rampant roosters was strutting towards the village of Astakos, crowing in a cocky manner and leaving a trail of vegetable devastation in their wake.

Chapter 51: Rampaging Roosters

"It's time!" Slick Socrates announced through a megaphone. "Stop dancing, bazouking and stuffin' yous faces with sardines. Mail order Masha is about to give 'er first weather broadcast."

An awed silence descended over the panagyri and all eyes were instantly fixated on the giant outdoor television screen. A round of spontaneous applause erupted as mail order Masha appeared on the screen in front of a backdrop of the map of Greece. Emulating the famous Petroula's provocative movements Masha managed to look super sexy while hardly bearing any naked flesh beyond her voluptuous silicone cleavage. Her long hair extensions shone a brilliant blond in the studio lights and she gracefully extended her bold red nail extensions to point at the different regions.

"She's a natural" her husband shouted with pride as Masha announced it was sunny all over Greece.

"'Ow can it be sunny when it's dark?" Nitsa queried.

"Dont's be so pedantic Aunty" Tall Thomas told her.

Finishing the weather report Masha announced the news section was about to follow and then sauntered off screen in a slinky manner that accentuated her silicone bottom. "Gets back on set" the producer could be heard yelling over the airwaves "yous will 'ave to read news too as newsreader 'as been taken ill."

The camera panned over to reveal the newsreader being violently sick in a bucket by the side of the news desk. The poor man had been overcome with stomach pains and nausea after greedily devouring two bowls of Masha's infamous borscht, laced with an almost toxic amount of vodka.

"Wow, it looks like Masha will 'ave to read news as well as doin' weather" Takis exclaimed. As the villagers remained transfixed with their attention on the television screen a disturbance broke out at the back of the crowd. The gang of escaped roosters, made up of Stavroula's and Quentin's unruly flocks, were following the scent of sardines and set off a raucous chorus of cockadoodledoos, pecking at ankles in order to clear a route to the food.

"Them fowls 'ave gone feral" Tall Thomas shouted as the squawking flock turned vicious. One malevolent male refused to release its grip on the hem of A Thousand Stork's ice cream smeared kimono, reducing the terrified woman to a blubbering wreck, whilst a randy rooster, attracted to one of Fat Christos' naked statues, refused to stop its shameless rutting antics against a plaster of paris model of Apollo.

"Elps me round 'em up and put 'em in coop" Stavroula screamed, throwing herself after a hen. Grasping the tail feathers, which came off in her hand, Stavroula fell in an undignified heap on the floor as the hen escaped her clutches. Quentin was fighting to maintain his balance as the parrot, still stuck firmly to his scalp, bobbed violently up and down attempting to attack the roosters.

Slick Socrates adjusted the volume on the television to its highest setting so as not to miss a word of mail order Masha's news presenting. Masha announced: "News just in of a breaking story of destruction and mayhem in the local village of Astakos. Over to our young reporter on the ground for live coverage."

Footage of the smitten young reporter replaced Masha on the screen and the camera zoomed in on the villagers desperately running after the marauding roosters. The smitten young reporter, spouting into his microphone, kept up a running commentary of the bedlam.

"Over the years we have covered many complaints from concerned residents of the region about the foul habits of roving randy rioters and the blight and devastation rampaging roosters reap as they ravage. Tonight we can witness firsthand the devastation wrought at the Astakos panagyri as innocent Japanese tourists are forced to take refuge in fishing boats. Here we can see a traumatised old lady cowering in the back of an old Mercedes taxi and a man of the church acting most out of character as he chases the runaway livestock, threatening to beat them to a pulp with his Bible. Oh gosh, I've never witnessed anything like this...." the reporter went silent as the camera lingered on a fight between the goats and the roosters.

One recalcitrant bird was trying to maintain its hold on Agapimeni's back, attempting to embed its claws into the knitted dress. Nero rushed to Agapimeni's rescue, using its freshly polished horns to butt the rooster off the rival goat's back. The bird flew through the air in an ungainly fashion, landing on the head of that old fool Vasilis who was cowering in fear by the side of Bald Yannis' shower curtain table. Incensed by this televised humiliation Vasilis grabbed hold off Bald Yannis' chainsaw and decapitated Stavroula's prize rooster live on air.

It was too late for the television channel to bleep out mail order Masha's final words as an accidental news presenter as she screeched "malaka, that old fool letting loose on roosters with chainsaw is my 'usband."

I Hope You Enjoyed 'Rampaging Roosters'

If you enjoyed this book and it gave you some laugh-out-loud moments please post a glowing review on Amazon and/or Goodreads and tell all your friends who love Greece and humour. Indie authors rely on reviews to help spread the word.

If you would like to be notified when the next book in the Greek Meze series is available please feel free to contact me on katerinanikolas@outlook.com

Katerina Nikolas

Printed in Great Britain
by Amazon